Contents

1943

Many countries were under German occupation. Many towns were completely destroyed by bombs. Many innocent people lost their lives in the countries occupied by the Germans.

One

_____AN ICY ROAD_____

I'LL never forget February 15, 1943, my first day in Germany. I was very young, just fourteen years old, when German soldiers, against my will, hustled me onto a train with nine other boys to take us from our home in Poland to Germany.

The journey was long, and we were tired, hungry and exhausted when we arrived in the town of Kitzingen. When we got off the train, a German officer met us and said, "Come with me." He escorted us through a tunnel into the station and turned us over to a man in civilian clothes.

Tired as I was, I spoke to this new escort in German. "Where are we going?" I asked, secretly hoping he would take us somewhere to eat.

"You speak German, so you should understand what I'm going to say," he said gruffly. "Shut your mouth and take longer steps so we can get somewhere."

1

I didn't ask any more questions. Scared, I tried to take longer steps.

A light snow covered Kitzingen, so it was chilly as we stepped out of the station and headed for town. I was not dressed for this weather. My boots weren't made for winter, and I had no gloves, no hat — just a fall coat.

The streets were icy, which made it hard to walk faster. The town had not seen any war. It was beautiful. No one else was walking, but there was traffic — bicycles, autos, horses, and buggies.

It seemed as though we would walk through the whole town. I noticed buildings of different sizes and shapes. Factories belched heavy smoke. Finally, we stopped at an old stone building. A sign outside said, "Register here."

We entered the building and a long hall with a high ceiling. "Sit on those benches," the German said, pointing. We did as we were told. Then, looking us over with a sharp eye, he took our papers, which were in envelopes fastened to buttons on our coats.

"I'll be in Room 102," he said. "You stay seated on that bench until I come out to tell you different."

We sat in silence. The building looked old. Many rooms opened on the hallway, and stairways led up to a second floor. Germans were hustling and bustling in and out of the other rooms.

Things were very quiet until what appeared to be a group of German civilians came out and chose the other nine boys to go with them. I was the smallest and youngest of the group.

"How come I wasn't taken with the other boys?" I asked myself. "Maybe they think I'm too young or too short." I became very nervous.

Finally, an older man came out of Room 102. He looked me over, then went back into the room. That made me worry even more.

After another wait, the German official and the civilian came out of the office. They both looked me over. The civilian looked like a farmer. A heavy-set man, he smoked a long pipe, which he filled while waiting and staring at me. The official told the farmer I could speak German. Then, he handed the farmer my papers. "He's yours now," the official said. "You may go."

The farmer addressed me. "My name is Schmitt. You are to come with me."

Schmitt and the official exchanged goodbyes, and the official returned to his office.

Outside, Schmitt took a big pull on his pipe and blew smoke into the air. Then, he said, "I hear you can speak good German."

"Not so good, but I can get by," I answered. "My father was in the first war. He had to speak German in Austria, so he taught me some German."

"I understand," Schmitt said. "You look like a very young boy. How old are you?"

"I'm just about fourteen years old," I replied.

"Good, good," he said. "We must cut this talk. We'll be on our way. Get up and come with me."

I grabbed my little package and followed him out the door.

The sun was shining, but it was still cold as we headed through Kitzingen's streets.

3

We had walked some distance, when suddenly a siren blared three times. People ran out of buildings, others left their vehicles, and they all headed for a bomb shelter.

"Come, we have to go into the shelter," Schmitt said, grabbing my hand and pulling me toward the shelter door. People huddled in the shelter for about fifteen minutes before the siren blew the all-clear signal. Someone remarked that it was going to be hard to stay alive through this warfare. I found out later that this had been an air-raid drill.

We came out of the shelter door almost past town.

"Do you know what country you're in?" Schmitt asked.

"I'm in Germany because the people speak German," I answered.

"You are in Kitzingen," he said.

We walked on. Then suddenly, Schmitt motioned for me to follow him into a cafe. I was hungry and tired from the journey, so I was happy to follow him. Schmitt hung up his coat and looked around. He spied two empty tables, took one for himself and told me to sit at the other one.

I put my coat and package on a chair, then sat down on another. I surveyed my surroundings. The cafe may not have been high-class, but it was very clean. It also held quite a few patrons.

A waitress approached and asked, "Would you like to order?"

"I'm sorry, but I'm with that man at that table," I said, pointing to Schmitt.

She turned to Schmitt and took his order.

4

I wished I could have ordered some food. I was hungry and couldn't remember the last time I'd had a good meal.

Schmitt looked prosperous, but he played cheap. The waitress brought him a meal and wine. Schmitt took out his wallet and paid. Then, completely ignoring the way I eyed his food, he took a sip of wine and began to eat.

His meal sure looked good. I felt depressed, so I opened my package and took out a loaf of hard bread and began to chew on it. I watched Schmitt, then gazed at the other people in the cafe. A pair of women at another table were looking at me. Schmitt, intent on his food, still ignored me.

One of the women, middle-aged and attractive, got up from her table. She placed a sandwich and a glass of beer on my table. "I can't finish these," she said. "You looked hungry and thirsty, so I thought you wouldn't mind finishing them."

"No, no. I wouldn't mind," I said. "Thank you so very much."

After so long without a meal, that meal sure was tasty. Better yet, Schmitt didn't interfere.

But after I ate, I felt tears forming in my eyes. I was very depressed. I looked at Schmitt, and he was just finishing his meal. He put some tobacco in his pipe. Then, he got up.

"Come along," he said as he put on his coat and hat.

Back on the street, it was warm enough that the ice was melting, but it was still cold and slippery. We headed down the road toward a big forest. Schmitt was quiet for a while.

5

Sometime later, he broke his silence, saying, "You're probably interested in where we're going."

"Not really," I said.

"My name is Schmitt," he said.

"You told me that when we met," I said. "You probably have a big farm."

"Yes," Schmitt said, "and we are going to that farm."

Both sides of the road were lined with pines — some huge, some smaller, all dusted with snow.

The winter sky was blue and clear, the sun bright.

"Are you hungry?" Schmitt asked all of a sudden.

The thought made my eyes water. I was so surprised I didn't answer him.

Schmitt took no notice and continued talking, "My daughter-in-law will have something good to eat at the farm." He paused, then said, "I'm sixty, so I can't work hard anymore. My wife died five years ago, and I am living with my son and daughter-in-law on the farm. They told me to get some help. That's you. You'll fill in for my sons, who are away at war. The government took all the young men and any man who was able to fight and left us just the sick and cripples. Even the able-bodied women had to go work in the plants and factories."

"Why tell me this?" I asked angrily. "I didn't want this war. You don't think I came here to look at the German countryside, do you? I know you have to work hard, but you German people wanted the war. You brought me here for forced labor. I thought you Germans were ready for war. Do you have a shortage of food or something? Do you have a shortage of land? So why ..."

"Shut your mouth or else!" Schmitt screamed. "Do you know what would happen if I turned you in? They

6

would either shoot you or put you in a concentration camp. Can you imagine what they do in a concentration camp? I'll explain it to you. When you go to the concentration camp, these people will destroy you. Either they won't feed you or they'll work you until you're nothing but skin and bones. Then you'll collapse. No water, either. You'll die, and then they'll put you in an oven and burn your body to small bones."

I shut up. Schmitt's concentration camp talk made me very nervous. I believed every word.

Soon after, we heard a vehicle approaching. It turned out to be a jeep carrying some special police. I was afraid that Schmitt would turn me in. I almost fell to the road in fear, but I controlled myself. I looked at the forest and thought, "This is my time to die."

Lo and behold, the jeep went right past as the men within waved at us. Schmitt made no move to stop them.

When the jeep passed, Schmitt looked at me sternly and said, "I was going to turn you in but changed my mind. Don't ever talk about our country again to anyone. Understand? Keep your mouth shut."

"Yes, yes, yes," I said. "You must forgive me for talking like that. I am so tired from the long journey I didn't know what I was talking about."

Acknowledging my fatigue, Schmitt said, "You'll make it. We're almost there. At the end of the trees, you can see my farm and village.

Soon after, we turned left off the main road. A village sat on the right side of the branch road. I could see a bridge ahead. Across the bridge stood a hospital with a very high clock tower. The clock had four faces, one in each direction.

As I studied the clock, it struck four.

The clock's rumbling chime sounded lovely, and you could hear it all over the area. That sound reassured me. I knew I would be all right again.

Schmitt must have noticed my fascination with the clock. "It is a beautiful sound," he said. "The clock is on the hospital in Schwarca. We are in the town of Schrcenau."

Soon, we were on the bridge. The steel span was very long and high enough to allow barges and boats to navigate the river below it. The river had sharp currents. It flowed west as it wound around the towns in the area.

"That is the Main River," Schmitt said, as he stopped to clean his pipe. He tapped the bowl against the bridge and ashes floated down to the river.

"It's beautiful," I thought as I looked out on the river and the surrounding countryside. The town was tidy. The houses and taller buildings like the local Catholic church and the hospital tower impressed me.

"In the summer, a lot of people walk here in the evenings," Schmitt said. "Soldiers come from the front and enjoy swimming in the river in summer. Even I come because it is so close to my farm."

He pointed to a house on a corner, "That is our house."

Soon, he opened a big iron gate, and we walked onto his property. I could see a barn for hay and stalls for cows. We entered the front door of his house. The house was not big, but it was clean and looked beautiful to me.

Schmitt matter-of-factly removed his coat and hat and hung them up. Then, he pointed to his daughter-in-law. She looked young, about twenty-seven years old, I thought.

Schmitt said, "That is Nina. Her two boys are Hans and Mike, and, as I told you, her husband is in the army."

Then, for the first time, he asked if my name was Stanislaus.

"Yes," I said.

"Come, sit by this table, and Nina will give us something to eat."

Nina took a few turns in the kitchen, putting some wood in the stove and warming up some dumplings and meat. She set plates and two glasses of homemade wine before Schmitt and me.

Nina stood to one side and stared intently at me, looking disappointed. Unaware that I could understand German, she said, "Papa, you brought us such a small child. He's too small for such a big farm."

"Yes," Schmitt said. "He is young, but he does speak German. He's also bright. He'll learn things easily. You won't have any problems with him." Then, he stopped trying to disguise his own disappointment. "I had to take what I could get. At least, I brought you help. You can't argue with that."

When we finished our meal, we sat for a little while the two boys, who looked to be about seven and ten years old, were doing their homework. That gave me an idea. I asked them for a pencil so I could write to my mother and father to let them know I was all right. The boys gave me a pencil. I thanked them and sat down to write in Polish:

February 15, 1943

Dear Parents,
   I wanted to let you know that I am in Germany. I will work for a German farmer. The town I am in is called Schrcenau. I am still alive and healthy!

   I got only that far when Schmitt asked, "To whom are you writing?"
   "To my parents," I answered.
   "What language are you writing?" he asked.
   "Polish," I answered.
   Then Schmitt screamed.
   "No! What do you think you're doing? I brought you here to work, not to write letters. Get up right now and put some work clothes on. You'll go to work right away. Nina will show you what to do. From this day on, Nina will tell you what to do! You listen to her and cooperate! If you don't listen, you know what will happen to you!"
   He dragged his finger across his throat like a knife.
   Nina spoke up then. "Now, you come with me. Take your package, and I'll show you where you'll sleep."
   So, I grabbed my package and followed her down a dark hall to a small room. It was well-kept, with a bed, chair, and a table by the window. I set down the package on the bed and pulled out some old clothes. As I put them on, I checked my bed and realized that I should get outside before I fell asleep. I hung my other clothes on the chair.

I hurried out of the house into the back yard, where Nina was waiting.

"Come with me, Stanislaus, and I will show you how to hook up the cows to the wagon," she said. "First, we have to push the wagon from the shed into the yard so it'll be ready."

When we got the wagon out, Nina led me to the stalls. They were made of stone and painted white. Within, I counted fourteen cows and two calves.

Nina pointed at two of the cows and said, "Those are our working cows. They'll work the fields and pull wagons and other equipment."

Then, she got out a yoke and showed me how to put it on the cows. We led the two cows to the wagon, which was prepared for a heavy load. There were heavy chains over the middle of the wagon, and in the front, a board acted as a specially made seat for the driver and passenger.

Nina sat on the board. She had a whip. A rope at the side of the wagon would help steer the cows. Nina held the rope and told me, "Open the gate. When I'm through, close it and come out to sit beside me. Then, I'll show you how to guide the cows with this rope."

"Good, good," I said.

When I got up beside her, she began to instruct me, but I began to nod off.

"Do you think I'm going to do this work?" the already disappointed Nina asked angrily. "It's not time to go to sleep."

I didn't say a thing.

We took the main road out to a gravel road by the river. From there, the view was very close to the first one I had of the clock tower, the river, and the surrounding towns. The remaining snow had melted, exposing the black soil.

"This view is beautiful," I thought. "I'll probably see it many times before the time comes for me to return to my parents — if my parents are still alive by then." I thought of how they might die in the war, and tears began to flow.

As the tears streaked my cheeks, Nina asked, "Why are you crying?"

"It's nothing," I answered. "Everything is OK."

Nina hung her head with a look of disappointment. She needed help, not a little boy.

"She's not satisfied with me because I'm so small," I thought.

Even so, she handed me the rope and the whip.

"Now, when you pull the rope to the left, the cows will turn left," she said. "When you pull the rope over to the right, they'll turn right. If you call out 'pyrr, pyrr,' they will stop right away."

She paused, then asked, "Did you ever drive cows like that back home?"

I had to laugh.

"No, no, never," I told her. "Only horses! We used them to pull plows and sleds. I've seen cows milked before, but I've never seen them used to pull heavy loads or plow the fields. That's murder on a cow on a farm this big. You should have a horse or a tractor."

A half-smile played on Nina's lips. "What do you know? You're too small to know anything, but let me tell you something. We can't afford horses or a tractor. All horses do when they're not working is eat up the pasture, and it costs a lot of money to keep the tractor running with rationed gas. Neither one of them can do hard work *AND* give milk."

I wanted to laugh again, but I didn't.

"The country has a war going, so the cow is still the cheapest and the best for these times," she said.

"Yes, yes. You have the right idea," I agreed. "You use your head."

Nina laughed because I gave her credit for being smart.

"Yes, yes. I'm still a young woman," she said. "I'm almost alone here to do the work. I have to think of ways to help myself. I have to think of the best way to do everything." A touch of bitterness crept into her voice.

We had reached our destination, a pile of rocks by the river. We got off the wagon, and Nina guided the cows closer to the pile. Nina explained that we were to load the rocks into the wagon. I began tossing these big rocks into the wagon, and Nina watched me fill it. I worked quickly, and we were soon on the road back to the farm. As we rode, we passed a few wood-fueled buses and bicycles.

Nina pointed out her land, and there were pools of standing water there. In fact, the whole area was very wet. She pointed to a knot of people in the distance, "You see where those people are working? That's where we're going."

As we approached the last hill, I again could see the hospital clock tower and the bridge over the Main. The clock tolled five, and the sound echoed all around us.

13

While I was caught up in the sight, Nina got off the wagon and got ready to push it uphill.

"Stanislaus, get down and help push!" she ordered. "This is a steep hill, so we have to help the poor cows." I got out and pushed as hard as I could.

When we got to the top, I could see what the workers were doing. They were hammering the rocks into three- or four-inch pieces and shoveling them out onto the road. Others were digging drainage ditches beside the road.

I found out that many of the workers were foreigners — Russians, Serbs, Poles, and Ukrainians — brought in as I was for forced labor. There were even French soldiers among them. These French prisoners of war were locked up at night in the local jail and worked on the farms by day. Some Polish prisoners of war also worked on the project, but when they were done, they were taken out of the area.

"Let's throw these stones to the ground," Nina said.

As I began to unload the wagon, I felt someone's eyes on me. I turned, thinking someone was going to ask me a question. Suddenly, I felt weak, and everything went black.

When I woke up, I was in Nina's barn, lying in a bundle of straw with the cows.

As I struggled to my feet, I saw that it was already dark outside. I walked to the barn entrance. Nina was standing outside.

"What is wrong with you?" she asked.

"I don't know," I answered. "Would you tell me how I ended up in the barn unconscious?"

"We put you in the wagon and brought you here," she said.

"Why didn't you bring me to my bedroom?"

"Because you didn't finish your work," Nina said harshly. "Get some beet greens and straw from the cellar. Chop them up in that machine over there, mix them all up, and feed it to the cows."

Then, she showed me the machine and how to operate it.

"When you're done with that, you can come into the kitchen for supper," Nina said.

I finished the chores and went into the kitchen. Dinner was waiting on the table. I sat with the whole family. The meal was meat and boiled potatoes, with bread, butter, and coffee. I took a small portion because I still felt weak, but I did finish it.

"Now, Stanislaus, you'd better get to bed," Nina said. "I'll wake you up at 6 a.m."

I was too tired to think about it. I said good night, brushed my teeth, washed my face, and went straight to bed.

It seemed just a moment later when Nina came in and said, "Stanislaus, get up! It's six o'clock."

After I washed and dressed, Nina sent me out to tend the cows. I fed them, spread some straw for their bed, and then it was time for breakfast.

The smell of coffee spread through the kitchen as I walked in. The breakfast was bread and butter. I ate well.

I did the same sort of farm chores day after day for months. Then, one day, Nina was very happy. She seemed so different, much more alive, less beaten down by her responsibilities.

I had never seen her that way before, so I asked, "Why are you so happy?"

"My husband is coming home on leave to see me and the family," Nina said.

A few days later, he arrived. It was early morning, and I was out doing chores. I heard he brought a lot of valuables with him, gifts for his family, beautiful things from different countries. I wondered whether he had bought or stolen them. The Nazi soldiers could do those things. Those who complained would be killed.

I met him later in the day, after he had lunch and took a nap. He came out and helped me hook up the cows to the wagon. We loaded the plow in the back, then went out to plow some fields for the spring planting.

When we got back to the house that evening, I was feeling sick and feverish, but I fed the cows before I went inside. I avoided supper and went straight to bed. I couldn't sleep, though, because my fever got worse.

Nina's husband woke me in the morning. I forced myself to get up even though I was very sick. I went out to the barn and collapsed on the straw. A calf licked my head. I moved away from it. I prayed for God's help. I wished that my mother could be there to help me, too. I spoke these thoughts out loud in Polish.

That's when Nina's husband walked in, and hearing me, he said, "What are you babbling about? Why are you lying down on the straw?"

"I am sick, very sick," I said. "I have a high fever."

He bent over me and touched my forehead. He said nothing. He just let me lie on the straw. Then, he did all my chores. He didn't even look in on me. I was pleased to lie there.

Finally, at noon, he came to me and asked, "Do you want something to eat?"

I said, "No, no. I can't eat anything." I was beginning to get nervous because I knew this little bit of kindness would end soon.

"Whether you eat or not, you still have to go into the field," he said. "My furlough is just about over, and I don't have much time to show you all the things I want you to do. You must get up now!"

Then, in a sharper voice, he said, "Come and sit on the wagon."

The wagon and the cows were ready to go. I tried to climb up, but I couldn't make it. I was light-headed. My head was spinning. The farmer gave me an angry look. Then he grabbed me by the shoulder and hoisted me onto the wagon with both hands.

The May weather was warm, and it felt good as the wagon trundled off to the field. When we got there, I tried to step out of the wagon, but the drop to the ground seemed three stories high to me. I took a few steps but fell flat on the ground.

Nina's husband came to me and was about to pick me up when I said, "I can't get up. Everything is spinning." He left me there and started the plowing himself.

I lay on the field for about two hours. I thought I might die right there. There wouldn't be any doctor for me. The farmer wasn't happy, but he probably understood how bad I felt. He hadn't even finished the plowing when he helped me back onto the wagon and took me to the house.

When we got there, he told me, "Lie in bed. In a couple of days, you will be OK."

17

For the next few days, all I could do was drink water. Before I got back on my feet, his furlough was over, and he had to report back to his post. He never had the chance to show me all the things he needed done.

Two

NINA AND THOMAS

THE nearby villages woke up from their winter slumber
that spring. Farmers and villagers were all busy, and
that's when I got the opportunity to get to know some
of them.

I had to report every Sunday to the Nazi mayor. This
was a rule just for the Polish laborers. We had to wear
a yellow letter P that showed we were Polish. We would
go to the mayor's doorstep, and he and an SS officer
would call out our names from a list and check them
off as we answered. That done, the mayor would tell us,
"I'll see you next Sunday."

Missing these meetings could mean jail, or
even death. The mayor had clout, and he could have
offenders shot or sent to jail or a concentration
camp.

Everything was going pretty well for me, until after
one of these Sunday reports, I met a fellow Pole named
Thomas.

"You know, Stashek," he said to me, "if you want to make friends with the rest of the Poles here, you'll have to put something on the table."

"What do you mean 'put something on the table?' " I asked.

"Your farmer was on furlough, and he brought home lots of merchandise, especially cigarettes," Thomas said. "That's what I'm interested in, cigarettes. Bring me some cigarettes."

"How am I supposed to do that?"

"Tell Nina that you want to smoke some cigarettes. I'm sure she'll give you some," Thomas said. "Then, you bring them to me."

"Look, you're not my friend," I told him. "You're a grown man, and I'm a child compared to you. You're just trying to take advantage of me. You want to get me in trouble. Besides, I don't want any cigarettes."

"You're being a smart ass," Thomas said. "Who knows when you might need my help? You've got no reason to be angry with me."

"Well, I don't know what I'm going to do," I said. "I might ask Nina about it, and I might not."

"Nothing will happen to you for a pack of cigarettes," Thomas said. "She'll probably give them to you, no questions asked."

I thought about it, and said, "OK, I'll try my best."

The next day, when Nina went with me to the field, I asked her for cigarettes.

"No," she said. "Cigarettes aren't for giving away. Someday, when my husband returns from the army, he'll smoke them."

A week later, I asked again.

"Could you give me just a few cigarettes to try?"

Nina didn't answer. She just turned and went into the house. I thought, "Well, that's that! I don't smoke! If Thomas wants cigarettes so badly, I'll tell him to ask her himself." I didn't mention the cigarettes to Nina again.

One morning a few days later, Nina came out to the back yard as she checked out the weather. "Listen, Stanislaus," she said, "with this nice weather, we'll go to the field after lunch and plant potatoes. Get everything ready on the wagon, and water the cows before we leave."

After lunch, Nina told me to go out and chop wood instead. That didn't make any sense because there was enough wood chopped to last about three years.

When I asked her why she changed her mind, she screamed, "No more asking questions! Do you understand?"

I wrinkled my brow because the change of plans and her reaction were so strange. "Something is wrong," I thought.

I took the ax and started chopping wood. As I chopped, I wondered what was wrong and what would happen. I worked steadily and soon had a big pile of wood chopped. I looked at the tower clock, and the hands showed one minute to two.

Then, I noticed two men were coming through the gate toward me. I recognized right away that one of them was the mayor. I didn't recognize the other, but he looked very strong. The mayor stopped by the side of the wood pile, but the other man came closer to me.

He said, "Throw that ax down and come here."

I did as I was told. As I did, I heard the clock strike two.

Then, the man started whipping me in the face.

He screamed, "I heard you asked for some cigarettes."

"Yes!" I said.

My face felt hot. Blood was running down it. I fell down on the wood pile, and he continued to beat me. I can't remember how many times he hit me. I could barely move, and still he kept on hitting and kicking me while I was struggling to hang on to consciousness. I heard the mayor say, "That's enough! That's enough."

The man stopped immediately. They walked out through the gate, and I heard it close after them with a squeak.

"I'm still alive," I thought, "but I can't move."

My face was so swollen and bloody that I couldn't see. Somehow, I managed to pull myself up to a sitting position. I rubbed my eyes and began to see daylight again. I looked at the sky. Then, I looked at my yellow shirt. It was no longer just yellow. The splattered blood made different designs on the shirt.

There was blood all over the wood I'd been chopping. I felt weak, and everything hurt. My flesh felt wooden. I couldn't move. I felt almost numb all over. I worried that I might be paralyzed.

I decided to see if I could walk. By using the neatly piled wood for support, I was able to get on my feet. I took a few steps, this way and that, still clinging to the wood. I was very weak. Finally, I sat down on the stump where I split the wood.

After some time, I got up and walked to the corner of the shed, where I had seen a broken mirror. I cleaned the dust off it.

I stared at my reflection, but I couldn't recognize myself.

Surveying the ugly wreckage of my face, I thought, "No. It's impossible that I'm still alive. God! God, thank you for the chance to go on living! You saved me from death. I'm not going to be a cripple! You were there with me through the whole thing."

I was thirsty, dehydrated from losing so much blood. Fortunately, I'd managed to stop the flow. I walked over to the water pump and began drinking, drinking, drinking. I don't know where the water went, I put so much of it away. Then, I pumped more water into a bucket and began to wash around my eyes so that I could see better.

The back yard was deathly quiet. No one was around. There was no sound from the house, either.

I don't know where the family was. The wagon stood untouched. I decided to go back to chopping wood but managed to chop only two pieces before I felt too weak to continue.

I looked around the yard for a good place to sit. I looked over at the shed, with its stacks of old wood. It took a little time, but I finally found a spot on a pile of wood and rested my head. I couldn't imagine why they had punished me so severely for such a small thing — asking for cigarettes. I tried to tell myself that I was fortunate not to be sent to a camp. After a while, I got sleepy and lay down.

I awoke the next morning.

Nina was walking around the back yard. I could tell she was scared to approach me. I didn't say anything, and eventually she gathered her courage and walked up to me.

"Stanislaus, come to breakfast. After we eat, we'll go to the field and plant the potatoes." She didn't look at me as she spoke, but I knew she'd seen my damaged face as I slept.

I got up and went in for breakfast. As usual, there was no one at the table but Nina. She set down the food and I ate. Afterward, we hooked up the cows to the wagon and got aboard. We were just about to start toward the gate when Nina looked at me.

"Stanislaus, before we go, maybe you should go and wash your face and change your shirt. It looks very dirty."

I had already rehearsed my answer in my head, so I spoke to her deliberately. "Yes, my dear young woman, this shirt is not dirty. It just has a lot of blood on it. You had a good look. Look at it again. It's Polish blood. You know where it came from. You also know you'll remember this day as long as you live. You can't forget that my blood is on your hands. So I'll just wear this shirt until it falls apart. It'll be a good reminder."

Nina sat transfixed. She didn't make a move to get the cows going. I continued, the words tumbling out easily. "Maybe the shirt will tell the villagers just how good Nina was to me. That won't help much now, but you deserve whatever comes from it."

I looked at her and saw her face had reddened. She wouldn't return my gaze. "I can see you are ashamed to be on this wagon. That's why you told me to change my shirt. I can see ..."

Nina threw the rope onto the wagon's floor and jumped out. I watched her run toward the house. Now that my tirade was over, I worried that she would turn me in again. "Now, they'll really finish me off," I thought. But I felt better for having given it to her. It was good to get my feelings out.

Before she reached the house, Nina called back to me. I asked her what was wrong. "You know where the potato field is," she said. "Take the wagon out there. I'll be there in a bit." She paused, then added lamely, "I forgot something in the house."

I watched her disappear inside. Then, I took up the rope and the whip and got the cows moving. "Vio, vio," I said to them. They moved toward the road.

As I rode toward the field, the gravel crunching beneath the wheels, I had time to think. It became clear to me that Nina wasn't the only one to blame for what happened. Thomas had a hand in it, too. He brainwashed me into asking Nina for cigarettes. Still, Nina had the biggest share of the blame. She had set a killer upon me for such a little thing. The man could have crippled me.

When we reached the field, I stopped the cows. I got down and pulled the plow off the wagon. I was so busy that I didn't notice Nina until she was right beside me. She handed me five packs of cigarettes.

"Take these," she said. "I should have given them to you days ago. I shouldn't have reported you to the mayor. Believe me, Stanislaus. I never thought they'd beat you so badly." She looked at me long and hard, almost crying. I wanted to accept her apology, but I couldn't.

"I thought they'd scare you a little bit," she said, shaking her head as if that would blot out the sight of my cuts and bruises.

"Thank you very much, but no, thank you," I replied. "I'm don't want those cigarettes, or any cigarettes. You know I'm not a smoker. I just wanted to give them to somebody else." That was as close as I would come to explaining they'd been for Thomas. Even though he wasn't a friend, I wasn't going to expose anyone to the beating I'd taken. Still, I was mad at him, too. It was very confusing.

"Well, you can give them to whomever you choose," Nina said. "You wanted them, so I'm giving them to you." She tried to put them in my pocket, but I pushed her off.

"No, no. I don't want your cigarettes. I never wanted them." Still confused, I tried to change the subject. "They look very expensive."

"Why?" she asked.

Then, something inside exploded and I shouted, "Because they cost me a lot of blood, that's why! Give them back to your husband when he returns."

Nina was fed up. Shaking her head, she threw the cigarettes into the wagon, where they spilled all over the floor in front of the seat. She started to work. We didn't speak a word to each other the rest of the morning. The silent work went quickly.

By lunch time, the potatoes were planted. I loaded the wagon and started toward the house. Nina, not saying a word, also set out for the house. In a moment, she disappeared from view. Suddenly, I panicked. "How is this going to look?" I thought. "Me, driving through town in a bloody shirt all alone. It'll be lunch time, and there'll be plenty of people out. What if they ask what happened?"

Sure enough, when I got to the village, some of the people pointed at me and began talking excitedly. "Who did you murder?" one asked, laughing.

I said nothing, pretending not to see them as I passed. Finally, I got to Nina's back yard, where I unhitched the cows and put them in the barn with something to eat. Then, I took more beet greens to the chopping machine so I'd have less work to do in the evening.

While I was busy with the beet greens, Nina appeared.

"Stanislaus, lunch is on the table. Come in." We usually ate lunch together, but today no one joined me at the table. Afterward, I went back out to water the cows and then to the field to finish plowing.

That evening, after I finished the field work, I made the mixture for the cows and fed them. I was thinking about going to my room to get a soap and towel to wash up. Instead, I found myself walking to the Main. The evening sky was so beautiful, still sunny, and the air was warm. The dried blood on my face began to fall off like seeds from a pod.

When I got to the river's edge, I felt confused about what to do. At first, I told myself, "I'm only going to wash my body, and I'll leave the blood on my arms." Then, I thought, "Nina's already seen my blood. It's time to wash it off." The cuts and bruises hurt so bad

I didn't dare touch them, and I continued talking to myself, trying to decide what to do.

Finally, I said to myself, "That's enough of this show. The best thing to do is wash my wounds in the fresh river water and let it heal me. Maybe even strip and take a bath."

So, I went back to the house for the soap and towel.

Because I didn't have a swimsuit, I got out of my clothes and into the water quickly. The June sun was still very warm, although it was setting fast. The sunset splashed different colors on the water. I looked up and saw the clock tower shining in the sun. It shone so brightly that I almost had to turn my head.

It took awhile to clean my cuts and bruises. While washing them, I marveled again that I was still alive. I felt very good all of a sudden, and began slapping at the water playfully.

Then, I saw somebody coming my way. I wanted to get my clothes on quickly, but I didn't want to step out of the river naked in front of him. Soon, I realized it was Thomas heading my way.

"How did he find out I was here?" I asked myself.

He lived a few houses down the street. He must have seen me come down to the river by myself.

"Maybe he's coming for his stupid cigarettes," I thought. "Well, I'll give him a good whipping." My anger was getting the best of me. After all, what could such a small boy do against this grown-up? I got so angry thinking about my size that I know if I'd had a gun, I would have shot Thomas then and there, without asking questions.

I was so worked up that I completely forgot the beauty and peace of the river that I'd been enjoying just minutes before. I definitely wanted to hit him, to hurt him. Then, I realized that I'd have to strike with words, my only weapon. My words would burn like fire. He would remember them as long as he lived.

Thomas walked closer and closer. I didn't get out of the water, though. I was still absently washing my arms while thinking about the damage I would do to him. About thirty feet from the river bank, Thomas started laughing and said, "I heard that woman Nina beat you up." Then, he laughed even harder.

That was too much for me to take.

"Why are you laughing, Thomas? Are you so stupid that you'd be a traitor?"

That stopped him. He looked at me quizzically. "What kind of traitor?"

"Come closer, Thomas. Come closer, and look at my bruises. If you were a true Polish patriot, you'd sympathize instead of laugh. This was a beating by Germans against a Pole."

I shoved my face closer to his, as he stepped closer.

"These cuts and bruises should be on your body, not mine," I said bitterly. "You're the one to blame because you have a taste for foreign cigarettes. Why don't you smoke them and tell me how they taste? That's the kind of Polish friend you are."

My words took effect. He backed away, still staring at my broken face.

"This is what they do to your brother for such a small thing as asking for a pack of cigarettes for a friend," I said. "I'm lucky I'm not a cripple now. But the beating I took is your fault!"

I enjoyed watching him squirm. "You see, if you don't respect your own people, you won't respect anything! Instead of trying to help your Polish brother, you're the kind of traitor who pretends to help, but instead ties a big stone around his neck and then pushes him into the water to drown. Traitors like you, Thomas, can be found everywhere."

Thomas was so taken aback, he didn't come over and bash me. So I kept it up.

"They are blind to their brothers' plight and end up nailing them down and handing them over to murderers. Yes, Thomas, it's happened more than once. That's your part in it!

"Believe me, Thomas! What's happened to me will one day happen to you. But why am I telling you these things? I'm just wasting my words. You'd better leave me alone now! I don't want to see you anymore."

I was as amazed by Thomas's reaction as he was by my tirade. He just turned and walked away without saying anything, his head down and his arms hanging loosely at his side. I watched him disappear under the bridge.

Then, I turned back to washing my hair. The blood was sticky, like glue, but my hair was short and easy to wash. I came out of the river and dried myself slowly, because everything hurt. Just as slowly, I dressed and started back to the house.

It was beginning to get dark. The moon and a few stars already hung in a vast sky. The moon shone so brightly that I could see the pebbles on the ground. I took a deep breath and felt clean again.

As I looked up at the stars, I thought about my mother, who had taught me how to spot the constellations. I looked up at the Big Dipper and many others — and felt at peace.

When I got home, I wrote a letter to my mother and went to sleep immediately. In a deep dream, I saw a woman walk up to my door and stand there. Then, I opened my eyes. The dream image was real. My room was dark, but I recognized Nina. I jumped to the door, put the light on, and saw her sneaking down the hallway. I caught up with her and grabbed at what she carried.

"What do you need my shirt for?" I asked.

"Well, I ..." she started, but I interrupted.

"Are you going to boil it down for soup? What are you going to do with it?"

"Nothing," Nina answered. "I mean, I was just going to wash it for you."

"At this hour? In the middle of the night?" I pulled at the shirt until it slipped from her grasp.

"You know very well that I don't want you to wash it. I'm going to wear it until it falls to pieces."

She said nothing but went straight to her room. I went back to mine and quickly fell sound asleep. In the morning, I got up and defiantly put the shirt back on and marched out to breakfast. I wore the shirt for three days.

That Saturday morning, the bells of the tower clock rang out eight o'clock, and the sound reached out to me across the fields. I was loafing in the back yard when I heard another sound — the squeak of the iron gate. The mayor and the killer who had beaten me black and blue were coming again. With them was a young lady.

All three walked directly to Nina's house. I got very scared. My heart pounded so hard, I put my hand on my chest to try to stop it. I knew time was running out for me now. They were surely here to finish me off or to take me to some camp. Nina's son Hans came out of the house. I ran over to him and asked if he knew anything about the two men.

"One's the mayor," he said, "and I think that my mom told me that the other one's named Kessler."

That was all Hans heard before they told him to leave the house. Later, I found out more about Kessler. He was a high-ranking Nazi, who hated foreigners and had a reputation for punishing them for small infractions. He particularly disliked Poles, ranking them not much better than Jews on his scale of hate. He sent Polish prisoners of war to the concentration camps whenever they refused to sign up for civilian work. He wasn't much kinder to others, either. From our area, he'd already sent two Frenchmen, three Serbs, and five Russians to the camps. Some said he made them cripples first.

Even without knowing all that, I was deeply worried. I dropped the garden tool I had in my hand and thought about running away. Instead, I asked Hans in a low voice so no one in the house would hear, "Can you find out why they came?"

"Oh, I know that!" he said, brightly. "My mother was talking that she was tired of you. She didn't like the way you act around the house, wearing that shirt. She said she didn't want to look at that bloody shirt anymore. She wanted to get a bigger man to work the fields. I think they want to set you up with another farmer."

I thought about the young woman who'd come with them. I couldn't get my hopes up, but maybe things would be OK after all. My heart stopped pounding so hard, and I thanked God. Still, I held my breath.

In my mind, I heard Hans's words again. "She said she didn't want to look at that bloody shirt anymore." I realized then that Kessler, who seemed to love beating me up, surely wouldn't stand for me walking around in a bloody shirt. I looked down and tried to brush off some of the caked blood. Maybe the shirt just looked dirty. Maybe Nina didn't tell him it was blood.

It didn't take too long to find out what happened.

Nina called from the back porch. "Stanislaus! Go to your room right now! Pack up your things! You're leaving us today!"

I didn't wait to ask questions but ran to my room. I quickly changed shirts and packed everything. I was all ready to go when Nina came in.

"Come with me," she said.

When I came out into the hall, I saw the mayor, Kessler and the young woman — a girl, really — were standing by the back door, talking. Kessler had his hands in his pockets. I couldn't see any weapon. The girl had her arms crossed in front of her. They were all laughing.

Nina went over to the girl and said, "I think everything is all set. You can take him now. His name is Stanislaus."

33

"I know his name is Stanislaus," the girl said and smiled. She was very pretty.

Then, the killer looked me up and down, his sour expression never changing. I wanted to look away, but instead, I looked at him intently. I got it into my mind that I wanted to be able recognize him someday after the war was over. My day for revenge would come.

I later learned that Nina got Thomas to take my place. I think that after seeing what a savage beating the Nazis gave someone so young, Nina came to her senses. She was good to Thomas. I think she learned something.

Three

————————ACROSS THE STREET————————

THE girl went out into the back yard and motioned for me to follow. "Come, we are going." I didn't say good-bye to Nina. I just followed the girl out. I was a bit taken with her. She was young, very pretty, and, best of all, about my height.

We crossed the road and headed to a three-story house, which also served as a tavern, post office, and butcher's shop. There, the owner made sausage, smoked meats, and bacon.

The girl led me into the house and introduced me to her parents, Mr. and Mrs. Sossa, and told them my name. Her parents leaned down to say good morning to me, and I answered the same.

Then, I asked the girl her name and whether she was the only girl in her family.

"My name is Guedraut," she said. "I have a married sister who lives in Wurzburg, and three brothers in the army. I'm the youngest. I'm only eighteen. How old are you, Stanislaus?"

"I'm fourteen."

"You're already fourteen?" the father asked in surprise. "Someone told me you were only thirteen."

"Yes, I was thirteen, but now I'm fourteen," I told him. "My birthday's not till the eleventh of November, but I'm fourteen now." I pulled my bloody shirt from my package and showed it to them. "This made me older. The day the blood ran down my shirt, I turned fourteen. This is my memory of my first step into a foreign country."

The house was suddenly silent. The parents just blinked and looked at each other. Then, Guedraut's father turned toward the front door and said, "Show him to his room. Have him put his things away. Then, we're going to cut some clover. It's too beautiful a day to waste."

Guedraut and her mother showed me to my room on the second floor. The room was very big. It contained an old-fashioned beer bar. A door in the room led to a big hall, which looked to me like a dance floor.

"This is where you will sleep," Mrs. Sossa said.

"How am I to sleep when people are here drinking?"

Guedraut answered, "We don't use that bar anymore, and we haven't had dancing since the war began. The saloon buffet downstairs is enough for the town now."

I put my package down and went downstairs. Sossa had already hooked up the wagon to haul the hay-cutting machine.

Sossa, Guedraut and I climbed aboard. Mrs. Sossa stayed behind to bake bread. We moved out on the paved road and turned off at the gravel road. The fields beside us were beautiful. At our left, an orchard of fruit trees — plums, apples, pears — was in bloom. On the other side, there was a vineyard.

The sight was so gorgeous. I was curious about who owned the orchard and how many acres were planted. Sossa told me there were more than six acres and that they were divided among seven other farmers. I took a deep breath, drinking in the wonderful aroma of the blooms.

Almost oblivious to that sweet smell, Sossa pulled out his snuff box and filled his nose. Then, he asked if my mother and father were still living.

"Yes," I said, "but they're old. My father is sixty-seven, and my mother is fifty-five. May I ask how old you are?"

The hint of a smile crossed his face. "I'm sixty-seven," he said, "but I feel very good. My wife is sixty, and she is also quite healthy."

Guedraut just listened to our small talk.

We passed a hill and arrived at the field where we would cut hay. We hitched the cows up to the hay cutter so that the blades would mow down the clover. Sossa sat on the machine, as I guided the cows to move in straight rows. Guedraut followed the machine, fluffing up the hay with a pitchfork so it could dry out more quickly.

We finished more than an acre of hay in a couple of hours. Then, we hooked up the wagon to haul the machine again and climbed on for the short ride home.

As we rode, I looked up at the tower to see the time was a quarter to twelve.

We got home, unhitched the cows, and hung up the harnesses in the barn. The barn wasn't very big, but it held four cows, including the two that hauled the wagon, and a small calf.

Sossa took me for a walk around the place. He showed me a hand-operated machine for cutting straw and another machine for cutting up the cows' beet greens and hay. He pointed out the hay and straw bins and showed me how to feed the cows.

Then, Guedraut called out, "Dinner is ready!"

Sossa started onto the sidewalk toward the kitchen and said, "Come on, Stanislaus, we're going in to eat."

In the kitchen, I sat down and looked around at the variety of vegetables and soup on the table. I was so hungry, my mouth was watering. Sossa and Guedraut passed the food to one another and filled their plates, but they didn't pass any to me.

"What's going on?" I thought. "How come they don't pass me the food?" I was afraid they wouldn't feed me. But I was wrong. This was the first time I was with them, and they did things differently from what I expected.

Mrs. Sossa picked up my plate and put some food on it. "Eat, Stanislaus," she said, as she put the plate before me. I ate every bit and was still hungry, but I didn't have the nerve to ask for more. I sat for a while by the table and then walked out back.

When I looked in the barn, the cows looked expectantly at me, so I figured they wanted water. I picked up a bucket and went to the water pump beside the barn. Bucket after bucket, I watered all the cows. Then, I took another walk to familiarize myself with the place because I was anxious to make sure I knew where everything was.

I wondered whether I could see the clock tower from the yard. It was barely visible from most spots, so I searched here and there for a clear view. I found a spot in the garden and felt a little more at ease. Knowing I could see the clock made me feel so different. I felt everything would go well.

When Sossa finished his nap, he had more work for me. Coming out into the back yard, he called, "Stanislaus, come help me! We've got to get the wagon ready to go to the brewery. We're going to pick up some fresh beer, but we have to load up the empty barrels first and return them."

He showed me how to load the barrels, using a big chain to hold them in place.

With everything just about ready, he said, "I have to put some better clothes on." Then, he looked me over and said, "So do you!" He said he didn't want people to see us in our work clothes.

"Can't people see us now?" I joked.

"Yes, yes. That's true," he said, "but we have to look better than this when we go out."

Still laughing at my own joke, I went upstairs to change.

Coming back down, I quickly opened the gate, and we headed back out onto the blacktop. We traveled about four kilometers along some tree-lined roads. Many people were out and about. We passed trucks, cows, and horses.

After watching them all pass by for a while, I asked, "How much farther to the brewery?"

"It's not very far," Sossa said. "This town we're going to is very old, but it's a nice, clean town. It's called Dettelbach."

"How often do you go for beer?"

"Oh, usually twice a week. Sometimes once a week. It all depends." Then, he changed the subject. "From now on, you'll be going for beer alone. Do you think you can handle that? These hills are so steep, you might kill the cows."

"Sure, I can handle it," I said. "I even feel better working alone."

Sossa got his snuff out again and put it in his nose.

"I don't own a very big farm," he said. "For me, it's plenty, though, because I have so much work to do. I slaughter the pigs and sell the meat, and I have a smoke house for the sausage, bacon, and ham. That's a lot of work. Even in winter, there's work, like making moonshine and cutting wood, of course. We need it to keep the house warm and to cook. I'd say we have work up to our ears."

The ride went quickly. As we started up a hill, I could see the entrance to the brewery. When Sossa parked the wagon, I threw the empty barrels where he told me. A man from the brewery helped us load full barrels onto the wagon. We left a spot for ice and loaded big chunks of it aboard. Then, we covered the ice with canvas so it wouldn't melt.

Back at Sossa's, we pulled up close to a large cooler beside the house. Sossa unlocked it with a big key that was always kept in the house, hidden for the family's use. The cooler was loaded with meat, beer, and other perishables. As we rolled the beer barrels into the cooler and unloaded the ice, the sight of all these provisions made me wonder how I could get into the cooler when I felt hungry.

"If I could get a good look at that key, I'll bet I could make a duplicate," I thought. "Maybe someday when I go for beer, I'll be able to take a very close look." Everything's possible when you're that hungry. A hungry person has to satisfy the hunger, and for all the hard work I was doing, they should have fed me more.

When we were done, Sossa locked the cooler and said, "We're all done here. Now, go unhitch the cows and take them to the barn. Then, come for something to eat. After that, you need to cut some straw and beet greens, because tomorrow is Sunday, a day off."

I did what he told me, then went to the kitchen for a snack. There was bread on the table, spread thick with good jam. Beside it was a glass of beer.

"Sit down and eat," Mrs. Sossa said. "You still have a lot of work to do."

When I was done eating, she told me to pick up a big basket and follow her. We went down to the cellar, which was built under the hay barn. She told me to go down the steps, get some beet greens, and carry them to the chopping machine.

I went down into the cellar. It was big and dark. The only light came from candles and a little window that opened up into the hay barn. They used that opening to dump the beets into the cellar. Looking around, I saw piles of beets and potatoes — and some old, big barrels.

41

I was very nosy. "Are they empty or filled with wine?" I wondered. Knocking on one barrel at the back, I found it was empty. I checked three more before I found one that sounded full. I pulled out a cork from the opening used to fill the barrel. I had no way of getting to the wine in there. "I wish I could have some wine," I thought. I could just taste it. I thought to myself how my grandfather once said that wine builds your blood. How I could use that now. "My goodness, all that wine!" I thought. "Is there any way I can taste it? If I can get to the cooler over there and to the wine in the barrel, I shouldn't be hungry or thirsty anymore. You know, I don't think I'll mind working with this farmer."

I tried to open the spigot, but it wouldn't budge. I looked closer and saw that it was locked. All the spigots were locked. I put a match to a candle and could see that I wouldn't be able to make a key for these locks. "All that wine, and I can't get to it," I thought. "There just has to be a way to get to it."

Then, I realized I'd spent a lot of time and I'd better get going on the greens. In a hurry, I filled the basket and was just about ready to head out when I heard someone coming. In walked Sossa, holding a glass pitcher. He went to a barrel and opened the spigot. As the wine poured into the pitcher, he asked, "Didn't you bring the beet greens up there yet?"

"Oh, I'm just coming with a full basket," I said.

Satisfied, Sossa carried the full pitcher back to the house. "He's probably drinking some of that wine," I thought. I took the greens to the machine and started cutting them up. Then, I cut some straw. The machinery was hand-operated, so I got tired. I was panting by the time I finished.

I hadn't come out of the barn yet when I heard Guedraut calling. I went into the kitchen and asked her what she wanted.

"Do you see the barrel standing there? That's where we put the water for cooking use. It's empty, and you have to fill it. Put that container up on your shoulders and come with me. I can show you where the water pump is."

Guedraut pointed to what looked like a bag with big shoulder straps near the big barrel. When I put the "bag" up on my shoulders, I could feel it was a barrel. Guedraut led me across the street to a big water pump. She told me to set the barrel on a stone that sat beside the pump. Then she began to pump water into the barrel. I listened to the water rush into it. The barrel filled quickly.

"Have you ever carried water before?" she asked.

"No. This is the first time I've tried," I said. "Please don't fill it all the way to the top."

She laughed. "I am a girl and I can carry the water with no problem."

When she finished pumping, she looked at me and said, "How are you going to carry the water?"

I put the straps over my shoulder. I lifted it a little off the stone, and then started walking. The barrel didn't feel heavy, but the water started to slosh out. By the time I had crossed the street, my shirt was drenched, and water was dripping all over my body. Guedraut was laughing her head off as she walked beside me. Water kept sloshing back and forth.

Sossa and his wife were watching from their window — and laughing, too. I stopped by the iron gate, thinking I could dump out a little bit of water and it would be easier to carry.

"Don't laugh," I told Guedraut. "How am I going to carry this up the stairs?" The water was so cold, I thought I'd freeze.

Her mother called out, asking what I'd said. Guedraut couldn't answer, though, because she was still choking with laughter. When she was able to squeeze out an answer, they all started laughing again.

It wasn't funny to me. I still had to go up the steps.

When I got to the kitchen, very little water was left. I came up to the big barrel and tipped the container on my shoulder. What I poured in didn't even cover the bottom of the barrel. So I had to go back down and get some more. I got better at carrying it each time. By the third trip, I was hardly spilling any, and, finally, I filled the big barrel.

Recovered from her laughter, Guedraut said, "You're not done yet. My papa said that you and I have to go out to the field, cut the grass down, and bring it home on the wagon."

We hitched up the cows and loaded the scythe, rake, and pitchfork. The field was toward the river, and we rode in that direction.

Before we got to the river, she asked, "Do you know how to cut grass?"

"Yes," I said. "Everybody knows how to cut grass. Of course, if the scythe isn't sharp, it's much harder to cut, but I know how to sharpen it if I have to."

Guedraut blinked her big blue eyes and laughed, but she said nothing.

I told her how good it was to ride on the wagon with her. So good, in fact, that I don't remember how long the ride took. I knew that I'd go anywhere with her and never get tired.

When she finally spoke, she said, "This is it! This is our field."

The field, farther from the bridge than from the house, followed the river for quite a way. Guedraut got the scythe off the wagon and started slicing through the grass. After a few passes, she said, "Now, it's your turn. I'm going to watch you cut the grass, because you'll be doing this by yourself most of the time."

She handed me a bull's horn filled with water. I hung it from my belt. She also gave me a whetstone to sharpen the scythe.

I sharpened it to a fine edge and then started swiping at the grass. She didn't compliment me on how good I was with the whetstone. She just took the fork and pitched the cut grass onto the wagon.

After a while, I stopped to rest. I took in a deep breath of good, fresh air, and I called to Guedraut.

She stopped and leaned on the fork. "What is it?" she asked.

"It looks like a beautiful night," I said. "I'm sure that you're going to go for a walk on the bridge. Do you have a boyfriend?"

"I do sometimes go for a walk — with my girlfriend," she said. "Boys I don't even think about! Maybe you haven't noticed, but there aren't any boys around my age. All of them are in the army!"

It was almost sunset. The clock showed it was just about eight. We raked the rest of the grass and put everything back on the wagon and started for home. At Sossa's, Guedraut got off the wagon and went in. I took care of the cows and put the grass away.

In the tavern, a lot of old farmers sat playing cards and drinking beer, having fun as they did every Saturday and Sunday night.

I gave the cows some fresh grass, spread some fresh straw in case they wanted to lie down, and headed into the house, my work done for the day.

ℱour

BROTHER AND SISTER

AFTER supper, I went down to the river to take a good bath after such a long day. As I neared the river, I looked up at the bridge, and something told me to walk across it and take a look at the river current washing by the pilings below. I walked out to the center of the bridge and, holding on to the metal rail, I leaned over to peer at the rushing water.

As I gazed down, a young boy approached me. He was shorter than I and German-looking. He placed his hands on the railing beside me and said, "My name is Joseph. Your name is Stanislaus. I've heard a lot about you. I saw you ride by my house in your bloody shirt one day. You were all bloody, face and all."

I watched him intently as he spoke.

"From that time on, I felt like I knew you, like we shared the same heart, because I lost my daddy."

"Your father was killed in the war?" I asked.

"Yes. My daddy was killed on the Russian front. We just got the message two weeks ago." Joseph's eyes welled with tears. He wiped them away.

"I'm very sorry," I said. "I know that's hard to forget." I knew what it meant to lose a parent. I'd lost two, even though, as far as I knew, they were still alive in Poland. My own eyes watered, and I was about to cry with him. "I won't cry," I told myself. "It's time to be a man, not a child."

Then, I told Joseph, "I can't cry anymore. I need to be a strong man, hard as iron, sharp as an ax. Nobody will help me but myself. I'm going to have to be my own guide through this time. I must travel through a fire that burns so hard till the day the fire dies. Some countries will get together and put the fire out, put it out with sand and water."

I pointed to the currents below.

"Joe, the currents of this river are mixed with human blood that is flowing through the whole world. My blood's in the river where I washed my cuts and my face. So is the blood of my brother, who was killed in Russia like your daddy. It flows with your daddy's blood and the blood of millions of different people whose blood has been spilled in this war. It flows in rivers and creeks.

"Don't cry any more, Joseph," I said. "You know it's not my fault or yours that you lost your father."

Joseph wiped his tears and looked me in the eye. "I know it's not your fault. There's one person to blame, the leader of my country — Hitler! Yes!"

"That's the truth," I said, "but how many people think like us?"

Joseph put his hand on my arm and said, "Well, all this talking! But now I have to go home. The sun is setting already. We'll meet again, though. I want to be your friend, if you don't mind." As he took a few steps homeward, Joseph asked when we could meet again.

"A friend? I doubt it!" I spoke cautiously and reasonably. "How are we going to be friends when you're German and I'm Polish. That's impossible. You could turn me in or get me in trouble."

We had reached the end of the bridge and continued to walk, along the river.

"Stanislaus, you don't understand me. I'm against the Nazis. I know they're going in the wrong direction. They're not going to win this war. Believe me, Stanislaus, I want to help you not betray you. You don't have to tell me anything about politics if you don't trust me. I can give you information about the war all over the world. I'll tell you where the Germans are weak. I'll even warn you if bad things are going to happen to you. You have nothing to lose."

We shook hands. He said, "We'll be good friends from today on."

I thought, "What will be, will be."

Joseph squeezed my hand and smiled. I smiled back.

"Don't worry about anything," he said. "Everything's going to be OK."

"My, oh my! Time flies," I said. "I've got to go to the river and take a bath." As we started to go our separate ways, I said, "I'm glad it's sundown because I have no swimsuit. I can't even buy a swimsuit anymore." I called out to Joseph, "Bye!"

Down below, I got into the water. Then I saw Joseph coming back. He sat on the river bank and looked at me as I stood in the water. For the first time, he saw the full extent of my wounds. "Oh, my God!" Joseph said. "You really got your face and body bruised up. Kessler beat you up, didn't he?"

"Yes, he whipped me as much as he could. It'll take quite a while before I heal."

"Yes, Stanislaus, it'll take some weeks or months before you're completely healed," Joseph said.

I finished my bath and dressed. Then, Joseph and I started for home. I asked him how old he was and how many people were left in his family.

"I'm eleven years old," he answered. "I have a sister and a very good mother. We live near the forest. You must know where it is because you've driven by so many times."

"I know that area very well," I said. "Is that where you live? About a kilometer from town?"

"Yes, it's quite a ways, but we like to live near the forest," he said. "It's such a beautiful spot, with the river flowing by. That's where I go to wash myself, too. I didn't plan to come by here today, but I'm glad I did because I wanted us to meet."

As we walked, I noticed reeds growing by the river. They were too big to break apart, but I knew they were hollow inside. Any one of them would make a perfect straw to suck up some of Sossa's wine. I took out my knife and cut off a thick, sturdy length. I was so happy to have a chance at the wine that I jumped in the air.

Joseph didn't know what to think. "Why are you so happy? What's that for?"

"I'm going to make a whistle," I lied. I didn't know him well enough to share this secret.

"Would you make me one like that, too?" Joseph asked. "How'll it look when it's done?"

"It'll look like a whistle," I answered. "You punch holes in the side, blow through the hollow part, and work your fingers on the other holes. I don't know if I can make it yet. It looks big for my use, but it'll be OK." I cut it into pieces and put it in my pocket, and told my new friend that it was time to go home.

"Are you scared to walk in the dark?" I asked.

"No," he said. It was just getting dark, so we started once again to go our separate ways. We couldn't do it, though. It was such a clear, beautiful night, with the crickets already chirping, I didn't want to go home. We started walking together in the direction of Sossa's.

Joseph looked up into the sky and said, "It looks very good for tomorrow. We're going to have a beautiful, sunny day. Since tomorrow's Sunday and you won't have to work, why don't you come to the river by the forest? I'll be there with my sister. I'll introduce you to her."

"No, no, Joseph! I probably won't come because I'm afraid. Don't you know we foreigners are forbidden to meet with German girls? Do you know what I'd get if someone saw me with your sister?"

"Yes, I know that you could be shot on the spot!" Joe answered. "It wouldn't just cost you your life. They'd probably shoot us, too. I've heard about that happening before. Don't worry, Stanislaus. Come by the river. There won't be anyone there except us. If there's any trouble, I'll take responsibility for everything."

"If that's the case, I'll come by," I said. By this time, we were almost by Sossa's, so we said goodbye again, and Joseph walked off into the darkness.

I opened the iron gate and entered the back yard. Nobody was there. Everyone was inside drinking beer and playing cards. I went quietly to the cellar. The door was open. It was dark down there, but I knew where the barrels were. I quickly put together the pieces of the straw. I groped my way to a barrel, crawled on top and pulled out the cork. I pushed the reed inside and sucked up some wine, relishing the taste. When I'd had my fill, I replaced the cork and crept out of the cellar. I shut the door, took my straw apart, and hid the pieces in the barn so I could use them another time.

The wine was good and strong. I made it upstairs, although my head was dizzy. I went to bed and slept it off.

The next morning I wanted to go to church, but we foreigners weren't allowed to go, even though I was Catholic and there was a Catholic church in town. So I prayed in my room and then wrote a letter to my parents.

After lunch, I reported to the mayor as I had to every Sunday. After seeing the mayor, the Polish workers would wander back to their villages. Many got together to play cards. All had some kind of plan for Sunday. I wasn't very friendly with them. I knew they were avoiding me. They were all dressed up, making like big shots. I was too young for them. So I sneaked away and headed toward the river to meet Joseph and his sister.

They were already at the spot where we were to meet. Joseph was swimming, and his sister was sunning herself on the river bank. As soon as he saw me, Joseph got out of the water and went over to his sister lying on a blanket. "Rita, this is my friend, Stanislaus," he said, introducing me to his sister, whom he said was fifteen.

I bowed to her and said, "It's very nice to meet you. You're a beautiful girl."

Rita laughed at the flattery. She rose to her feet and said, "Well, you don't miss a thing. How old are you?"

"I'm fourteen," I answered.

Rita sat down and asked, "Aren't you hot standing there in the sun? Take your clothes off, jump in, and cool off."

"Sure, I'm hot, but I can't get in the water," I said, "I don't know how to swim."

"Oh, I'm not a good swimmer, either," she said. "Just get into the water and stay close to the bank."

I backed off a few steps and took off my coat and shirt because it was hot. The spot they'd chosen for swimming was lovely. The river bank was lined with stones, and pine trees crept up near the grassy bank where Rita and Joseph had spread their blankets. About ten miles from the river on the opposite bank stood another pine forest. It could be seen from afar like the mountains and the small town.

Right there, the river rushed with a strong current. From time to time, barges and boats would pass, but right then, we were alone — just us and the birds singing in the forest, all secluded by the pines.

Rita — so young, blond, and good-looking — made the scenery even better. So I sat on the grass, close to her blanket. "Does your mother know where you are and who you're spending this lovely Sunday with?"

Rita turned to face me. "Yes, Mother knows where we are, and she knows you're with us. Don't worry about her, though. She's not your enemy. She was supposed to come with us, but she had too much work to do at home."

"It's very nice that you don't keep secrets from your mother," I said. "That proves you listen to her and respect her. I hope you never have to find out the way I did, how much your mother is worth to you."

What I said caught their attention. Joseph, who'd been lazily plucking at grass, said, "Since we're talking about my mother, why don't you tell us about your mother? How many are in your family? And most important, why did you leave them to come to Germany?"

Rita looked at Joseph, then at me, and said, "Yes, tell us about your family and how you got here."

They seemed to think I came to Germany on my own.

"Since you're ganging up on me, it looks like I'll have to tell you more," I said. "It's a long story, and I'm not sure I can translate it clearly into German, but I'll try."

"Don't worry about your German, we understand you very well," Rita said.

"Good, good. Give me a few minutes because I don't know where to start. I have so much to tell you."

I thought for a minute or two and then began:

As you know, I'm Polish. In Poland, I lived by a forest just like you do. It was big pine forest — acres of pines, blue spruces and oaks. The pines looked like candles rising into the sky. The oaks were so big in diameter that it would take nine men holding hands to reach across one. Wild animals like deer, wild pigs, and foxes roam that forest. So do forest mice and ground hogs, porcupines, lizards, rabbits, wolves, and snakes of all kinds.

The forest held animals of all colors — red squirrels — and all kinds of birds — pigeons, owls, eagles, crows, blackbirds, quail, and ducks. Some birds migrated from the south, like the wood stork, with its long legs and black-and-white wings. The woods were full of martins and cuckoos, too. Black gulls made their nests in the fields, and some birds migrated all the way from South America.

The forest was alive with blueberries, cranberries, blackberries, raspberries, strawberries, mushrooms, and hazelnuts. There were all kinds of wildflowers there, too, and the scent of them made you feel so alive. A big river flowed through this forest, a home for fish and frogs. That's why birds came to nest there.

The forest was a joy. The best toy I ever had when I was a kid. I was always busy there. To me, climbing high trees was a big sport. Once, I brought home a little fawn and had to feed her and take care of her. I trained two blackbirds to sit on my shoulders. I had babied them since they were small, so they'd always come to me. That was fun.

I also used to fish, and picked berries and hazelnuts in the forest, too. They were all so sweet. I'd even bring *wildflowers home. I knew all the animals' nests and lairs. In the winter, I'd go out into the snow and trap rabbits and bring them home for Mama to make rabbit stew. At Christmas time, I would travel far through the high snow to find a spruce tree for Christmas Eve. It wouldn't matter how blustery the weather was, I had to get the tree. So, I'd take an ax or a saw into the forest searching for the right tree.*

I never was afraid to go into the forest. I'd been going there since I was seven.

And close by my house, there was always something to do, too. In winter, I'd go ice skating and sledding. Those were my sports.

My dad was a big farmer. He owned many acres. Fruit trees and a garden circled the house. My dad could afford to hire workers. Our buildings were nice and clean, even the hay barn. We always raked and swept the back yard.

There were nine of us in my family — my dad, mother, older brother, five sisters and me. We lived all together in my dad's house. We lived very well, and we always had enough to eat. My dad always threw parties for the family, relatives, and friends. It seemed he was always inviting people to come for beer, wine, whiskey, and as much as they could eat.

The village I come from is called Konczyce. A road cut through the forest led to a big town called Rudnik. Nearby ran the beautiful San River. It was lovely to walk through the trees, with their strong scent and the birds singing, especially when the cuckoo was at his best. Did you know cuckoo birds lay their eggs in another bird's nest so that the other bird will feed the babies? When the baby cuckoos are old enough to leave the nest, that's when the adult cuckoo takes over.

On Sunday, we'd walk to church in summer. In winter, we used horses and a sled. Sometimes, we'd use the wagon. All year long, we'd take the wagon out to buy and sell things. We also went to the movies from time to time.

I was always busy in the fall, when I'd take the horses to the pasture. I'd start in the morning, making sure to pack some potatoes, carrots, beets, butter, and bacon. I'd ride my own horse to the pasture, leading the other horses out there. I wouldn't get home until dark.

When I got to the pasture, I'd let the horses in. Then, I'd pick up branches to start a fire. I'd get a nice one going, sit down for a while, and then I'd go look for mushrooms. Many times, my friends brought their horses to the spot, too. Sometimes, there'd be quite a few of us.

The Jarat turpentine factory was in Rudnik, and we could hear its whistle sound each day at 8 a.m., noon and 4 p.m. Jarat was a big factory that employed many people. Its whistle wasn't very loud out in the woods, but it was audible. The noon whistle would be my signal to put some more branches on the fire and to put some potatoes and carrots beside it to bake. Red beets were dessert. I'd put the bacon on a spit and hang it over the flames. I'd watch the food, turning it over with a special stick as it browned. I'm telling you, those were delicious baked potatoes — even better with butter. Everything tasted good out there — the bacon, the carrots, the beets.

When the factory in Rudnik sounded the shift change at four o'clock, I would pack up everything, put what food was left in my bag, and head home.

At home, we had piles of wood, even boards from the sawmill in Rudnik, handy for cooking and heating. Beautiful flowers were planted around the house, and the garden was full of cucumbers, tomatoes, lettuce, rhubarb, carrots, corn, cabbage, cauliflower, radishes, and beans of all kinds. Everything we needed for the kitchen was stored in our cellar and the store room. In the cellar, crocks were filled with milk, sour cream, butter, and curd for cottage cheese. We even kept jars of jam down there to stay cool. We filled big barrels and crates in the store room with wheat and flour. Dry mushrooms, smoked bacon, and sausages were all hung in there. In the henhouse, the nests brimmed with eggs. I had to carry a huge basket to collect them all. The barn was full of hay, and I used to love to sleep there in the summer because the fresh hay smelled so good.

Yes, we were very proud of our farm. We never wanted for anything. Everything was fine until the Germans declared war on Poland. German soldiers took everything away from us, right down to bread and butter. They took the wheat, the pigs, some chickens, geese, ducks, and our cows. We only had two. When they took our horses, they left a half-dead steed as a replacement.

We weren't the only ones who suffered. They took everything they could from all of Poland. They even took the bells from churches. Everything they took went by train to Germany. When they'd cleaned up all our possessions, they started chopping down our forests for timber. The pines, the oaks — all they left were the stumps. That wasn't enough for them. The Nazis then started taking people and sending them to hard labor in Germany. They were like dinosaurs that ate or destroyed everything in their paths.

Soon, they were putting civilians in jail, even shooting them. I think the dinosaur was a bit scared that someday the people would turn against the Nazis, blowing up in the monster's belly as if it had swallowed dynamite. I think that's why they started transporting so many people to Germany so quickly. They tried to destroy our nation's identity. They destroyed our emblems and burnt our flags, even those in our homes.

As all these terrible things happened, all I could do was look out the window and watch our good life slip away. Without our horses, we couldn't plow the fields. The Germans imposed high taxes, which became more costly to us as our farm became less productive. Slowly, all the goods we had stored disappeared. The wheat was just about gone. We were out of potatoes and butter. The milk was almost gone. We had two pigs left, but the Nazis would have put us in jail forever if we had slaughtered them.

All this took its toll on my parents. My dad was getting older and couldn't work as much as he used to. My mother was heartsick waiting for my brother to come back from Russia. He never did, and we never found out how he died.

I didn't finish school because my oldest sister and I worked at planting new trees in an effort to make some money. My other four sisters would help Mother here and there around the house because they were still small. We kept out spirits up, though, working for the future, helping each other and working together, to get through Hitler's time.

One day, the mayor of our village was told that the Germans were taking over a big territory that included Konczyce. We would have to move and take everything with us, unless we wanted to volunteer to be Nazi slaves forever.

It seemed impossible that we could get out of there with everything. There was so much to be packed up from the farm. We packed what little had been planted— wheat and potatoes — before we lost the horses. My dad had no choice but to spend some money on a horse to help transport the food and our belongings.

Daddy rented us a house in Rudnik. He also rented a barn, where we could store what we took from the field and house the animals we had left. We had maybe two months to take care of all of this, but somehow we managed to transport everything by wagon to Rudnik.

And that's how we came to February 2, 1943 — Candlemas, a holy day in honor of the Virgin Mary, a holiday in Poland. That was the day the Germans captured me from church. They brought me to a big building in Rudnik, near the San River.

Like an omen, the candle burning at home sputtered so much wax that it snuffed the flame. That's when Mama heard the news that I'd been taken, and she began to cry. My parents were told that I was among many captured who would be sent to Germany for hard labor.

We were being held at that building by Gestapo guards, waiting for transport. Hearing the news, my *parents found their way there to try to see me one last time. I saw them on the street, while the Nazis took the names of everyone who was captured. My parents looked half-dead.*

It was just about dark when the Gestapo took us out of the building and back onto the street, where they lined us up. They trained machine guns and lights from their vehicles on us so that no one would escape in the dark.

A group of tearful parents stood some yards away, and among them I saw my father and mother again. They managed to get close enough to me to say that this was the last time we'd see each other. They wiped tears from their eyes. Under his arm, my father carried a package he'd packed for my journey. To give it to me, he moved through the prisoners. For his trouble, a Gestapo guard hit him in the chest with the butt of his rifle. My dad slipped in the snow and dropped the package. It slid across the snow toward us. When I saw that, I took a few steps out of line to pick it up, and quickly returned to the line. That was a big risk. The Nazis had announced that anyone who stepped out of line would be shot on the spot. Fortunately, the nearest guard just looked at me without speaking to me or hitting me.

My dad got up and faced me, shook his head from afar and gave me a slight smile to let me know he was OK. I knew I'd taken a big risk, but I figured Dad had risked everything to get me the package. Why shouldn't I take the same risk to pick it up? I knew they'd feel a little better about my going if they knew I had some food and other belongings with me.

We were all young people in line — young men, young girls. I appeared to be the youngest and smallest one they took that day. Many had been taken from Candlemas services that morning in the villages and towns around Rudnik. The Nazis even went house to house looking for young people. When the Gestapo came into the homes, they'd ask, "Where are your older daughters and sons? Are you hiding any Jewish people?" If they didn't find anyone at home, the Gestapo would ransack the house, looking for something to steal, like gold and jewelry. They picked on little children and old people. Many were killed with rifle butts.

Everything happened so quickly and unexpectedly, it was difficult to gather things to take along. Still, many of us had suitcases or packages as we waited in line. It was difficult to say goodbye to our parents. Rudnik was virtually silent. Nobody talked. The faces were very sad. People just counted the minutes until we'd be taken away.

The Gestapo, though, talked together in different languages, croaking like frogs in the spring. Suddenly, they screamed.

"March! March ahead!"

The line started plodding toward the railroad station. We left behind our footprints in the snow. Our parents watched us go and waved goodbye. Tears ran down their faces. As the tears hit the snow, they melted it with a little sound. So many tears fell, it sounded like bees in a hive.

No one tried to escape. There was no chance when there were so many machine guns around us. The lights from the Nazi trucks, reflecting off the snow, made it bright as day, so there was no place to hide, either.

A *passenger train was waiting for us at the station, and the Nazis ordered us aboard. By morning, we reached Krakow under a heavy Gestapo guard. The Gestapo ordered us out of the train there and marched us through town and over a bridge on the Vistula River. We were taken to a tall building in town, which was also guarded by the Gestapo. The building's huge halls made me think it had been a courthouse. These halls were packed with people waiting for transport to Germany. It was difficult to get by one another in the halls. We slept on the floor — men and women, packed like sardines.*

After a few days, our group was put on a train out of Krakow. The train made few stops. We were guarded by a number of the same Gestapo officers who picked us up in Rudnik, just fewer of them. This made it easier for us to talk to one another. Some said they might try to jump off the train, even though we didn't know where we were or where we were going. As the train was taking a curve, I was able to look out a window and count the cars in this transport. I counted twenty-six. In three of the cars, I could see women staring out of the windows. Two steam engines struggled to pick up speed to help pull the overloaded train uphill.

All the seats were occupied, and many people were standing by the door of the car. I was lucky because I had a good seat by the window. However, as I watched the last miles of Polish soil go by, I didn't feel lucky. I was depressed. I thought about how many times Poland had been attacked or taken over by neighbors hungry for our soil, which was like gold.

As we headed west, I was surprised to see that the snow had melted in these parts. I could see the day was clear, and the temperature felt warmer. It was almost noon, and the talking on the train was growing louder and louder. People were talking about jumping.

"Gentlemen," one said, "this is our last chance to jump! It won't be very long before we're at the German border! Then, it'll be too late!"

"Yes! This is our chance," said another. "There's only one Gestapo guard on each car."

A third said, "This is a beautiful spot to jump. There's a grassy slope down from the tracks, and there are bushes we can hide behind."

Yet another man chimed in, loudly, "People are jumping! Even women! This is no joke! It's real!"

Of course, when the people started to jump, the machine guns started to talk along the length of the whole transport. Our car was getting less crowded. About fifteen boys had jumped from it. Men and women had jumped from other cars as well. They were heroes to us. They all deserve medals. They risked death because they didn't want to leave Poland.

Joe and Rita listened very carefully, without asking questions. They were so intent on the story that they forgot to put suntan oil on their shoulders. When I saw how red they were getting, I stopped my tale to tell them they should put something over their shoulders.

"We'll have to stop now, for sure," I said. "This story is too long to be told in one day. Go to the water, cool yourself off. Your backs are red, very burnt."

Rita got up right away and said, "No, no. Don't stop! Keep talking. We'll put some oil on our backs to protect us."

Joe said, "You can't cut us off like that. You have to tell us what happened on the train."

"I'm not going to continue until you get in the water. I'm a little tired from the sun and all this talking, so I'd like to rest a little bit."

"That's good," Rita said. "We should take a break, but promise us you'll finish the story later."

"Don't worry, I will."

Joe and Rita went to the river and swam by the bank. I lay down on the blanket. I didn't want to go into the river, because I had no swimsuit. I didn't look for shade, for I love the heat from the sun. I thought about how Rita had started to like me. When I was telling my story, she looked right into my eyes.

I didn't notice her coming out of the river. She had cupped her hands full of water and poured it over my neck and back. I jumped up off the blanket and turned to her with a little smile.

"Wow! That water sure is cold! Are you that cold, too?" As I said it, I grabbed her by the ankle and she fell onto the blanket. Joe sat down, too, and asked me to finish my story. So, I continued:

What happened to the young people who jumped off the train is very hard to say. I'd guess that not everyone made it. The spot was very clear before you reached the bushes. I wanted to jump, too. When I opened the door, I peeked through the opening and two machine-gun bullets ricocheted off the steps and the door. I fell back, and the train's motion blew the door shut. I crawled on all fours back to my seat. My whole body was shaking like a leaf on a tree. Thank God, I was moving

65

cautiously. If I'd made the jump, I probably would have been shot.

As I sat there, I thought, "Oh God! How dangerous life is, and how short it can be." I had cheated death by only a tenth of a second.

Then, a new fear crept into my head. Would the Gestapo come looking for me? The Gestapo guard behind the machine gun had probably seen me and would recognize me. Then, I told myself, "Don't think about it. Just wait to see what happens."

The others in the car kept looking at me, knowing what I had tried to do. Most of them said nothing about it. However, a middle-age man sitting beside me leaned over and whispered, "Young man, if I were you, I wouldn't try to jump a second time. The Gestapo are mad as dogs. Besides, we're already over the border."

I said nothing. I just hung my head. The man was right. I'll remember that moment for the rest of my life. I didn't look at him because I felt ashamed.

The others were looking out the windows and talking to each other. I heard someone say, "Yes, we've crossed the border. We're already in German territory." We said our goodbyes to our homeland and prayed that, with God's help, we'd one day return.

At that moment, I wanted nothing. Nothing would please me. Very sadly, I looked out the window once more. Then, I set my head against the frame and closed my eyes for what I expected to be a brief rest. Instead, I fell immediately into a deep sleep.

I dreamed that I was on the newest, most beautiful train, riding in first class. The seat was very comfort able, with new springs and cushions. On the wall, buttons were labeled: beer, whiskey, lemonade, steak dinner. Curious, I pressed one of the buttons to see if they'd work. Out of the wall popped a bottle of dark beer! I whistled to myself and thought, "This is some technology!"

The train was moving like an arrow through the countryside, and its sides glistened like a mirror in the sunlight. All of a sudden, the train stopped. I looked out — and there was the back yard of my home in Konczyce! Dressed in a fine suit, I got off the train and shook hands with my family.

My dad said, "Is that you, my dear son? I knew you'd come. That's why I built this track, so you'd have an easy path to get here." Then, everybody pulled me into the house. My body felt heavy, like I was over weight, so heavy I felt I couldn't even walk. But nobody cared, they just dragged me in. I screamed, "I can't! I can't! Leave me alone!"

Then, I awoke. The man next to me had his hand on my shoulder. He shook me and said, "Get up! Get up! We're getting out."

Everyone else was standing and slowly filing out of the car. I got up and put the package under my arm and got into line. We had stopped at a very small station. It was dark. I couldn't tell what the name of the station was, or whether there was a town nearby. All I knew was that we were in Germany.

There were no Gestapo here, just some kind of police. They lined us up and led us through a forest on a wide gravel road. There wasn't any snow, but it was very cold that night. They marched us at least three kilometers before we reached some barracks surrounded by a barbed-wire fence. I figured it was some kind of camp or jail. In the center of camp, a light stood atop a post as tall as a telephone pole. The camp was silent except for a few whispers.

It was 5 a.m. when they put us in the empty barracks. They were cold. There were wood stoves inside but no wood to be found. Everybody shook from the cold, from hunger, and from lack of sleep. Oh, I wouldn't have wished this trip on my worst enemy.

Tired, we sat huddled on the floor for two hours. There were no beds or chairs anywhere.

As the sun rose higher in the sky, the light slowly crept up to our barracks windows.

The high command of this camp wore uniforms that were different from the Gestapo's. They looked like butchers. One of them took two men from our barracks and told them to get some wood for the stove. When they finally got the fire started and the room began to warm up a little, the Germans chased us into the field. The butchers told us to line up. They screamed and hit us with billy clubs, trying to hurry us up. They beat us up if the line was crooked. I'll bet they broke half of their billy clubs over our bones. Then, they took us to the mess hall, where they gave us soup — a most delicious breakfast. It was just beets cooked in water, really not very filling. Then, they marched us back to our barracks.

This pattern continued for days. These were the longest days of my life. At times, I felt like giving up. The butchers treated us like cattle going to the slaughter house. They beat us up constantly. They'd hit us wherever they wanted, in the head, in the ribs, any where. They even kicked us and used their fists. Things *were worst whenever they lined us up. That's when they beat us the most.*

If someone couldn't put his shoes on quickly enough for them, they'd rush into the barracks and push him out shoeless, even though there was frost on the ground and it was very cold. You know how cold it is in February.

Where is the respect for human rights? Or is there one set of rights for Germans and another law for every one else? The Germans feel they are the only race in the world. Maybe you can find a polite word for them, but I don't think they deserve any medals for the way they treat everyone. Let's call them what they are — killers and thieves! Out of meanness or out of jealousy, they beat up on anyone who's not German. They always attack other countries and take all their gold. They melt the gold into bars and put the bars into their cellars for their own future use!

Suddenly, I caught myself and looked at Rita and Joe. "I don't know why I'm telling you all this! You didn't do anything to me. I've got to quit talking now."

Rita thought about this for a minute. Then, she said, "What you said didn't hurt us. We understand your feelings. You have the right to express yourself, to be angry at the way you've been treated. You've only told this to us, and you don't have to worry. We won't report you."

"My father told me never to be afraid to tell the truth," I said, "but how far can I go in this country with the truth?"

"That's a good question," Rita said, "but, sooner or later, the truth will surface. The time will come when the Nazis will lose their power. Someone will pry open the iron door that hides their secrets. They'll tell the truth of what they saw with their own eyes!"

Joe piped up. "Please, Stanislaus, finish your story."

"There's still much more to the story," I said. "I'll only go on if Rita says OK."

"Of course I do," said Rita.

I shifted my position on the blanket and told the rest of the story:

One day I was so unhappy, so depressed and hungry, that I couldn't stand still. I started pacing the barracks. Time moved slowly. I asked someone with a pocket watch for the time. It was 10 a.m. I took the last remaining food from my pack. Some dry bread that Daddy had taken so much trouble to give me. The bread crunched audibly as I chewed. Ashamed of my bad manners, I went outside to eat.

People were walking back and forth by their own barracks. I leaned on the wall and crunched my bread, taking in the clear weather. A light breeze moved the pine branches. As I looked at the barbed-wire fence, I thought about having to line up again. I was sick of the line and the brutal discipline. I began to shake with anger. "I'd like to get out of here as soon as possible," I thought. My thoughts turned to running away. Which corner would be the best to make it through the fence?

As these thoughts passed through my head, two camp guards walked by. They were speaking in German. I stopped crunching so I could hear what they were saying. After all, any information might be helpful

to me. *They said that the prisoners in Barracks No. 4
must go through a doctor's examination because the
next night they would be shipped all the way to Bavaria.
This news made me very happy, even though I was
housed in Barracks No. 11.*

*I said nothing to anyone. I planned to go to Barracks
No. 4 and get out of the camp. I figured that there were
so many people in the barracks that the Germans
wouldn't know the difference. I went inside No. 11,
picked up my package and began to tie it up. A
young man walked up to me and asked, "Young boy,
would you give me a piece of your bread? I'm so hungry,
I don't know what to do with myself." I told him
there wasn't very much, but that I would give him
some.*

*"This bread is dry and hard," I said. "You can't cut it
with a knife."*

*"No matter what kind of bread it is, you were eating
it, so I'm sure I can, too," he said.*

*We held each end of the bread and broke it in half.
He took a piece and gave me the rest.*

*He thanked me eloquently. Then, he added sadly,
"You know, I couldn't take anything with me, and I
didn't get to see my parents either. They don't even
know where I am. They didn't see me go."*

*I could see he wanted to talk more, but I had to cut
him off because I wanted to sneak into Barracks No. 4
as quickly as possible. I picked up my package and
went outside. I stopped for a moment by the door to see
if any guards were coming. Luck was with me; there
were none in sight. I knew the other prisoners wouldn't
talk, even though they would have no idea what I was*

doing. *So I walked slowly toward No. 4. It was quite a distance, but I got there without a hitch.*

I walked into the barracks and sat down like I belonged there. I pretended like nothing was up. Some other prisoners looked at me, but they said nothing. Within the hour, camp guards came in and began taking names, making a list of everyone in Barracks No. 4. They counted everyone two or three times and counted the packages everyone had. Then, they took us through a gate into a different camp.

We were told to put all our packages to the side. We were in a hall with ten barber chairs. Everyone sat down and waited for the German barbers to clip our hair almost to our scalps. Then, we were told to leave our packages behind and were taken to another hall. Here, we were given baskets and told to put all the clothes we were wearing into them. Our names were written on the baskets, and when we put our clothes in them, we were told to pass them through a window. The people on the other side put our clothes through disinfection. They also gave us claim numbers for the baskets. We were taken to a room with twenty showers. There were about one hundred forty of us, so we had to take turns. The water was nice and warm at first, but then it went icy, so we rinsed off fast. Then, we had to wait in a cold hall, naked, for about forty minutes before we could see the doctors.

We were almost blue with the cold. We ran back and forth to get warm. The building started to shake, and the wooden floor creaked from our running. This angered the guards. One stormed in and addressed us in broken German and Polish: "Do you think this is a dance hall or something?"

"Sir, we're very cold," one man said.

"Cold! Our soldiers at the front are cold!" the guard said angrily. "Be quiet! If I have to come back, I'll bring a billy club with me." Then, he left.

Finally, we were let in to see the doctor. That room was warm. The examination was fairly routine until the doctor asked us if we were Jewish. He examined our penises carefully, looking to see if we were circumcised, for few non-Jews were circumcised.

When we were done, we retrieved our baskets from the window and dressed. Then, we were taken to another barracks. This was different. It had wooden beds, with clean pillows and two blankets apiece. I lay down and took a deep breath. I thought, "Oh, my God! This bed feels so good after all those nights sleeping on cold, dirty floors." I was very thankful that I knew enough German to understand what those guards had said, otherwise I'd still be in Barracks No. 11. "It'll probably be another two months before the people in my old barracks are moved," I thought, "but I'll be out of here tomorrow. I don't care where I go, as long as I get out of this hole."

I rested a bit, then they called us for lunch. The meal wasn't much of a change, but it was a little better. They added potatoes and other vegetables to the beets. It was passable. The important change was in their stupid system. They didn't chase or beat us anymore. They didn't line us up anymore. The other camp was torture, but here I felt like a human being again. We were still being held against our will, but we were clean, with new haircuts and a medical exam to boot.

Back in our barracks, everybody talked happily to each other. Then, a bitter note was sounded.

"When we went to the doctor's, I counted one hundred forty of us," one man said. "Now, I count one hundred thirty-four. That means six boys are missing." He wondered aloud whether they didn't pass the examination. Perhaps they were sick and taken to another barracks, which was the most hopeful explanation. Then, he said, "Maybe they were Jews, and they were taken away."

"That's probably it," said another man. "In this place, we can expect anything, even death."

Another man asked, "Does anyone know when we're going to be shipped out of here?" Somebody answered that it was hard to tell when we'd be leaving or where we'd be going. I knew the answers, but I wasn't sure I should tell them.

Finally, I said, "I heard we're going to Bavaria, and we'll be shipped out tomorrow evening."

A fellow sitting on a bench said, "You don't know anything about when we're going. Where did you get such nonsense? You probably made it up."

He said it so meanly, that I had to answer him. "I don't know what hour, but it'll be tomorrow evening. You don't have to believe me. We'll see tomorrow, if we're still alive."

I said no more and walked outside. I knew they didn't take me seriously because I was just a small boy. I just dug my hands into the deep pockets of my pants, put my head down, and walked around outside the barracks, waiting for sundown.

Actually, it seemed as if all I had been doing since the Germans took me was to wait. I wished it would turn dark so the next day would be that much closer.

When the night finally came, I went to bed. Yet, as tired as I was, I couldn't sleep. So it was a long wait until sunrise.

"The day has come to get out of here," I told myself at the first rays of dawn. Then, the hours dragged by again. I waited and waited, and still no word came about our move. Finally, sunset reddened the sky. Then, sunset began to give way to darkness, and we still hadn't heard anything. "What could have happened?" I asked myself. "Did I misunderstand them?" Everything else the guards had said turned out to be true. "How am I going to show my face around here if we don't leave? I said we'd be out of here tonight! What am I going to tell these people?"

They may not have taken me seriously, but they remembered my words. The man who criticized me the day before soon approached me. "Well, young man, when is this trip going to take place? Where is that Bavaria, young man? The only place you'll see Bavaria is on a map!"

I didn't know what to say. Then, finally, I just told him what I thought. "Sir, right now we're waiting for the train."

He turned his back and walked away. I only made that answer to satisfy him. I had no idea what was going on. A moment later, though, a camp guard came in and told us in broken Polish to pack up our belongings and come out of the barracks.

The barracks was a flurry of traffic as people hurried to get things packed. Excited to get going again, we all packed quickly and hurried out the door. Within ten minutes, all one hundred thirty-four of us were outside, ready to march wherever we were told. We waited in front of the barracks for a couple of minutes, then four police guards showed up and gave the order:

"Forward, march! Forward, march!"

It was almost completely dark as we marched down the road to the railroad station. We waited there a little while, then the train came. Three cars were empty, and we were told to board them. It was a third-class passenger train, carrying German civilians in the other cars. The train left as soon as we were aboard.

The police hung envelopes with our identification papers from the buttons of our coats. The envelopes were tagged with our names. We traveled through towns big and small, but I wasn't interested in their names anymore.

We traveled all that night, the next day and night, and into a second day. I didn't care about the stations we stopped at, but I was fascinated by the other transports we passed. I couldn't take my eyes off them, trying to glimpse the people they held.

Some we'd pass as they waited for a clear track, others would pass us. I saw hundreds of them. Some carried tanks, cannons, and other military vehicles and equipment. Others carried wrecked planes, food trucks, cows, pigs, horses, coal, wood, and other cargo.

I saw first-class passenger trains loaded with German soldiers drinking whiskey on their way to the Russian front. I also saw transports headed west, returning German soldiers from the front — one soldier was missing a hand; another had no legs. Many had their heads bandaged. Others had frostbitten hands, ears, feet, or legs. Many had casts on their limbs.

76

Russian prisoners of war were shipped in cattle cars. I could see them peeking out through the narrow spaces between boards. They all looked frozen and hungry. Their beards were long. When I looked into their eyes, they were begging for help. At one station, I heard a Russian say something I'll never forget. "Water, water, water," he said, the Russian word sounding so similar to the Polish that I understood him. His pathetic request stuck in my mind and made me have sympathy for them, especially when I thought about how many thousands of miles they had traveled in cold cattle cars. I'll bet they never had a meal aboard those trains. I saw they didn't have many clothes on them, so I know they were cold. Sometimes, I saw the Germans open up the cattle cars and toss dead men out.

At about 5 p.m. of the second day, our train stopped at Neustadt. Ten of us and the German guard assigned to us transferred to another train. The rest of the men from Barracks No. 4 marched toward the town. Without any food, we waited in the station for two hours before our train arrived.

It was another third-class passenger train filled with German civilians. Since we only took up ten seats, we traveled in a car with some civilians. We traveled the night through and arrived in Kitzingen at eight the next morning.

"That's how and why I came to Germany."

Joe looked at me intently. A boat moved up the river. Then, he said, "Stanislaus, I wouldn't wish the journey you made on anyone."

They talked about how they had heard all kinds of stories about the horrors of war through newspapers and books, but how nothing they'd heard so far could match the story of the brutal treatment that I had endured.

"Your story touched our hearts," Rita said. "It's hard to believe, but the most educated people in Germany let themselves be hypnotized by that maniac Hitler. It happened so quickly. The German people just turned their backs on God and forgot about loving our neighbors. Don't despair, though. Polish people may have lost their homeland, but they didn't lose their soul. There are millions of Polish soldiers scattered across many countries, fighting against Hitler."

We talked some more about the politics of the war, about how an agreement forged by Polish General Sikorski with the Allied leaders — Roosevelt, Stalin, and Churchill — got many Poles out of Siberia, where they were treated harshly by Stalin, to Iran and then to England or Mexico. Rita told me that many of the men went to England, signed up for military training and were fighting under Sikorski's command, and that most of the women and children were sent to Mexico for their safety.

Rita said that the German news told a slightly different story. It said that Sikorski made the agreement only with Roosevelt and Stalin. In addition, it said that Sikorski argued that, since his Polish soldiers were fighting on all fronts, he wanted Poland to be free from Stalin. According to this report, Sikorski was sent by plane on a secret mission with his daughter, who was a doctor, and a pilot, who was also Polish. After these three took off, their plane crashed at sea. Only the pilot survived to tell the story. The plane had been sabotaged by the English or the Americans, the Germans said. Churchill and Roosevelt didn't want Poland free, the German report said.

Rita told me that the Germans and Italians had been pushed out of Africa. "Their grasp on the world is shrinking, and that's good news for you, Stanislaus!"

"Rita, do you think Poland will be free after the war?"

"That's a question mark," she said. "It's a little too early to know what will happen to Poland. It's almost certain that Germany will lose the war. That'll end the German occupation, but what will other countries do after that? Who knows? I know, though, that if Germany wins the war, you'll never see Poland again. You'd be a slave here the rest of your life. So would millions of others across the world."

"That's true. Oh, God! Don't let the Germans win this war," I said. The thought almost scared me.

I thanked Rita for filling me in on news from around the world and for giving me a chance to express all the thoughts I'd stored up since the Germans invaded Poland.

"Thank you for sympathizing with me," I said. "I don't know what I can do to return such a favor." Then, I told them how much talking like this meant to me, and I hoped we could have many more Sundays like this one.

"Don't worry, Stanislaus," said Joe. "There'll be plenty more Sundays. We'll meet here. Nobody knows the place, and we can talk freely."

Rita echoed his thoughts and then added, "But now we must go home. Take care of yourself, Stanislaus, until next week."

We said our goodbyes, and I went down to the river. When I got to my room at Sossa's, my thoughts were filled with Rita. She was very impressive. Someday, after the war, we'd get married and we'd travel around the world, even to Poland. I already knew how to make love, what love means, and why people marry. I felt like I was in love with Rita.

Five

HITLER YOUTH

MONDAY morning came, and it was back to hard work for me. It was so hard to get started, with six days of labor ahead of me.

Sossa, Guedraut, and I cut the hay together. We turned over the hay. We raked the hay. We pitched the hay onto haystacks. We baled the hay. We threw bales on the wagon to bring them to the hay barn. On Saturday, we got a break from this routine because the afternoon was stormy. Fortunately, Sunday dawned bright and warm.

I set off again to meet Rita and Joe. It was still early, so I decided to walk to the bridge first. I was dressed down a bit, and I took off my shirt as I walked. The tower clock chimed eleven as I reached the bridge. No one else was on it, so I stood there soaking in the sun. I held on to the railing and leaned over, fascinated again by the strong currents below.

I was just about to head for the river to meet Rita and Joe when I was surrounded by a group of Hitler Youth. I don't know where they came from, but seven teen-age boys had circled me. I'd seen them before. They were from the surrounding villages, and they dressed up every Sunday in their junior Nazi uniforms, bayonets hanging from their belts.

One of the older boys, who looked to be about eighteen, asked me, "Do you know how to swim?"

I didn't know what to say, but I knew I was in big trouble.

Still, I didn't feel very afraid. I looked him in the eye and said, "Why do you want to know?"

Then, they jumped me, screaming. They held me by my hands and feet, and one said, "Let's throw this Polish dog into the river." They picked me up, but I struggled with all my strength. I kicked one of the boys so hard that he fell. He lay on the bridge as the others continued to hold me. I tried to run but couldn't escape their grip. I felt them lifting me over the railing to throw me in the river. I grasped the railing, but they threw my feet over. I lost my grip and my balance and almost fell. Somehow, I reoriented myself and grabbed the bottom rail. I hung there, looking down at the water about fifty feet below.

The monsters didn't wait long to renew their attack. They began jumping on my hands, trying to make me lose my grip. I couldn't hold on much longer with that pounding. I figured my chances of just dropping into the water and swimming to shore downstream. I wasn't a good swimmer, but I was losing my strength just hanging there. I tried to maneuver out of range of their feet, but I couldn't because my pants had fallen down in the brawl, and they'd tangled up around my ankles.

The devils couldn't reach me with their hands while standing on the bridge, so one crawled over the railing and, hanging on to it, reached out to cut me with a bayonet. The others were laughing because my pants fell down. I saw the bayonet coming closer and tried to move out of its way. Then, the devil cut me.

Instinctively, I pulled my hand off the bridge. That was too much. My other hand gave way, and I fell into the water. I sank like a stone. I swallowed water, but I kept kicking my entangled feet, trying to come back up to the surface. I broke through and sucked in the air, blood still running from my fingers.

Far above, the Hitler Youth were laughing. The current had pulled my underwear down to my shoes, too. "Here, we'll throw your shirt down! Catch it!"

Another shouted, "Hey, he's drowning! He doesn't know how to swim!"

"Too bad," their leader yelled. "Let the dog drown!"

While they were having their fun, I was struggling to keep afloat. I couldn't move my feet much with my clothes tangled around them. I was moving downstream fast and feeling weak. What kicking and paddling I could do wasn't moving me closer to shore and safety. I kept the presence of mind to realize I needed to disentangle my feet.

Somehow, I managed to grab a shoe and pull it off. The current pulled the clothes off that leg.

As I reached for the other shoe, I went under again and swallowed some water. When I broke the surface again, I saw I was still bleeding. The blood made a thick, cloudy trail in the water. It looked bad, and I almost lost heart. But I kept kicking and paddling until finally I got the other shoe off, and the pants and underwear went with it. Being naked was the least of my worries. The clothes hanging from my feet felt like a stone, dragging me down. Now, I felt I could maneuver to save my life.

The river was taking me to a bend, where I knew the current would be stronger. In my exhaustion, the river looked as big as the ocean. Still, I put my last drop of strength into kicking and paddling toward the shore. It didn't seem to be working. My vision was blurry. I couldn't see the river bank and couldn't tell what direction I was moving.

In this spot, the current pushed me to shore. My head and hands reached shallow water by the bank, and I began to crawl. Then, I fainted. I lay there for some time. When I opened my eyes, I felt water covering me up to my waist, one elbow sat in a little puddle, and my hands were splayed out on the river rocks along the bank. Some of the rocks were dry and warm in the sun.

I looked at my hand, and the blood flow had slowed. I saw that, somewhere along the line, I had cut my knee, too. I sat down and stared out at the rushing river. I turned my gaze back to the bridge about a quarter-mile away, and then I pondered the river's currents. "I'm lucky to be alive. God helped me for sure."

There was no one around. I walked naked across the grassy bank until I came to some bushes. I hid behind them and tried to decide how I'd get back to Sossa's. I thought of waiting until dark. The tower clock chimed two o'clock. No, it would be too long to wait till dark. I thought about taking the trail along the river to Sossa's house because no one appeared to be walking on it. Then, I realized I could fashion a wicker skirt for myself out of the twigs from the bushes. I was handy with wicker work because my brother taught me to make baskets.

As I was working on my skirt, I saw a girl approaching on a bike. I stooped down behind the bush so she wouldn't see me naked. Maybe I could ask her for help. As she came closer, I recognized her as Hilda, one of the girls from Sossa's village.

I called out to her without shouting. "Hilda. It's me, Stanislaus. I need your help!"

I'd scared her. She jumped off her bike and started to run. I called to her a little more loudly. "Don't be afraid! I won't hurt you! I'm sure you know me. I work at the tavern for Sossa."

Hilda turned toward me, still unsure, and asked, "Is that really you, Stanislaus?"

"Yes, it's me."

"What are you doing here? You scared me something awful!"

"I'm very sorry, Hilda, but I had to stop you because I need your help badly. I was up on the bridge when the Hitler Youth attacked me and threw me into the river. I don't know how to swim, but I managed to get to the river bank here. I lost my clothes in the river, though. I have nothing on right now."

"Why are you so far from the bridge if you can't swim?" She still didn't trust me, I guess.

"I didn't swim. The river carried me here. I almost drowned."

"What kind of help do you want from me?"

"Do you know Guedraut, Sossa's daughter? You must know her."

"Yes, yes. I know her."

"Good! I'm begging you, please ask Guedraut if she could bring me some clothes so I can get back home."

"OK, I'll do that right away," Hilda said. With that, she jumped on her bicycle and sped off.

Because I expected Guedraut to be coming for me, I threw the pieces of the wicker skirt into the river. I talked to the river. "You are powerful and clean. Take this skirt instead of me. Take it wherever you want and then bring me good news – bring me my freedom."

Soon, another bike approached. It was Guedraut, all dressed up for Sunday. I stooped behind the bush and waited. As she neared the spot, she got off her bike and began to call, "Stanislaus, are you there?"

"I'm here, Guedraut!"

She threw the pants on the grass and got back on her bike. "Thank you," I said, as politely as I could. "Thank you." When she left, I quickly put on the pants and walked barefoot to the bridge. I was on the opposite bank from Sossa's. Some crippled soldiers, patients at the hospital, had come out on the bridge. They got out there every Sunday in summer, taking walks by the river and even visiting Sossa's tavern. I ran quickly across the bridge and up to Sossa's back gate.

Guedraut was in the kitchen, and I asked her if she had any bandages for my cuts. I showed her my wounds. She asked, "How in the world did you cut yourself like that?"

I told her about how I'd been jumped by the Hitler Youth on the bridge and how I ended up behind the bush on the river bank.

"Who were these boys? How many of them were there?" she asked.

"They're from the villages around here, so you probably know them. There were seven of them."

Guedraut named them one by one, and I said, "You got it. That's them."

She took a bandage from a drawer and wrapped my cuts. "Do you want something to eat?"

"No, I'm not hungry, just exhausted from the fight and being in the water. Could I have a glass of beer, though?"

Guedraut poured me a glass at the bar. I drank it and went upstairs to my room. I lay down on the bed and fell asleep immediately. When I awoke, it was Monday morning.

Like always, it was back to work. Working was never good, but sometimes it was just plain lousy. This was a lousy week, but I finally made it through to Sunday again.

When I reported to the mayor as usual, he asked me, "Where were you last Sunday? You didn't report to me!"

I told him that I didn't report because the Hitler Youth had jumped me and thrown me into the Main to drown.

This made the mayor angry at me. "How did you get mixed up with those boys? Don't you know the Hitler Youth are Hitler's favorite children? Let this be a lesson to you – something to help you remember."

Then, he struck me – four strong blows to the face. We were standing in his front yard, and the force of this beating knocked me over a little fence. Blood ran all over my white shirt.

He stopped hitting me and said, "That's all for today. You can go now."

As we all left, I heard Thomas laughing quietly, although it sounded loud to me. He was still mad at me over the cigarettes.

Out on the street, a tall, strong Polish man whom everyone called Big Stanislaus spoke angrily to Thomas. "Is this a big laugh for you? How can you laugh at a Polish brother who's bleeding? He did nothing wrong, you idiot!" He almost hit Thomas in the face.

I didn't stay to watch their argument. Instead, I headed over the bridge and walked to the police station in the next village. There was an Austrian police officer there to whom I could talk. He wasn't in, though, so I kept going down the road to Kitzingen.

I wanted to find out if I had any rights at all. I remembered the town and walked to the police high command. At the desk, I told the officer that I was a very young child, I worked very hard for no pay, and, on top of that, everybody felt free to beat me up.

"See how I'm bleeding. A week ago, some Hitler Youth threw me in the river to drown. Two months ago, Kessler almost beat me to death, and now the mayor beat me up for no reason. I didn't do anything wrong. I didn't bother anybody."

The officer got up from behind his desk and walked around in front of it. "Why are you here? What do you want from us?"

That scared me. I thought he would beat me up or shoot me on the spot. You could expect just about anything from these police.

Somewhere inside, though, I found the courage to speak. "Sir, I would like to be transferred to a different village or a factory. I'm a good worker. I'm a human being, too, and I have a family that I'd like to see again someday."

The officer paced the floor with his head down thoughtfully. Then, he turned to another officer.

"What do you think?"

"I think it might be best to transfer him," the other said. "We have plenty of jobs around here. We could even put him in a factory."

"That's good. So maybe something can be done. First, I have to check with the mayor in Schrcenau."

This gave me some hope. I couldn't believe they were treating me so well, listening to me without screaming at or hitting me.

The call to the mayor changed everything, though. The mayor laid down the law and said I would not be transferred. He told the officer that Sossa had three sons in the war, and he needed me to work for him.

The officer gave me a note and told me, "Go back home! On the way, stop at the police station in Schwarca." That was the place I had stopped on the way to Kitzingen.

So, I headed down the road for home. I walked slowly. I figured they were going to lock me up in

Schwarca because I went to Kitzingen. We foreigners weren't allowed to travel freely into the big towns. I reached into my pocket and pulled out the note. I couldn't make out what it said because it was smeared. So I put it away.

I was getting close to Schwarca, when I turned to the left and went down to the river. I found the same spot where I'd saved myself. I sat on the grass, took off my shirt, and took in the sun. I didn't want to get to jail too early. I didn't want to waste this beautiful, sunny day. I washed the blood off my face and hands and then relaxed.

I sat there almost till sundown. Then, I got up to go to the police station in Schwarca. When I got there, I pretended to be hurt so I'd have an excuse for taking so long to report. The police from Kitzingen probably called and told them to expect me.

"What took you so long?" the officer at the desk asked.

"I twisted my leg along the way. I had a hard time walking."

He didn't ask any more questions. He just took me downstairs to a cell, put me in and locked the door. It felt strange to be locked in there by myself. It was the first time in my life that I'd been in jail. The cell was small, with a cement floor, an iron door, and a barred window. A bed made of boards stood by the wall. I was very hungry, but the officer didn't bring me any food. I was pretty sure they'd let me out in the morning. They wouldn't keep me here when I had to work. I sat on the bed for a while. Then, I figured I'd better get to sleep. I just tossed and turned. The bed squeaked all night.

When sunrise finally came, the officer came downstairs, opened the door, and asked, "How's your leg?"

"My leg's better. I think the boards helped straighten it out!"

"Good," he said.

We went to the yard behind the station, and he took out his bicycle. Then, he walked me over to Sossa's. Sossa was in the back yard by the cow stalls when we arrived. The officer explained what had gone on. Sossa probably already knew I'd been in jail. When the officer left, Sossa told me to go inside to change and get some breakfast.

I hadn't eaten since about eleven o'clock the previous morning, so I changed quickly. Guedraut served me breakfast, as she always did. I ate and went out to work with Sossa.

On a Monday evening two weeks later, I was coming back to Sossa's from a walk along the Main. Dressed in street clothes, the same seven Hitler Youth surrounded me. Quickly, I darted between them and ran to the back yard. I shut the gate and went to the shed where I had a three-foot stick ready. I hefted it and headed back out to do battle.

I wasn't afraid of them, even after what they did to me before. I didn't care that it was seven to one, or that I'd probably end up in jail or a concentration camp for fighting them. "What will be, will be," I told myself. "I'd rather die in a camp than back down from these little Nazis." I just wanted them out of here.

I pushed open the gate and rushed to the middle of the street like a mad lion, swinging that big, thick stick. They'd been trying to sneak up on me in the back yard, but we didn't see each other. When they realized I was out on the street, one screamed, "There's that dog."

I whipped the stick at him. I didn't care where I hit these guys, just anywhere I could reach. The stick broke in half, and the biggest boy sat on the road, clutching his leg. I kept on swinging at the others with the piece of the stick that I held. One of them took a swing at me with the other stick and hit me on the shoulders. The group grabbed me and held me. I was getting tired. They were winning, but I kept up the fight.

From an open window, Sossa's wife watched with a big smile on her face. She'd seen the whole thing and said nothing. The Hitler Youth hit me again and again. They tried to get me on the ground, but I kept hitting back.

They screamed, "Kill the dog!"

One went to hit me over the head with the stick. I stooped, and he only hit my shoulder. I felt like falling to the ground in exhaustion. I was sure they would kill me.

Then I heard Guedraut shout, "Leave him alone! Get out of here! Go home!"

The boys immediately stopped beating me. Some grabbed the injured boy and started to run home. Guedraut yelled one more time. "Go home, you gangsters!" The rest of them left, and the street was quiet. I was bent over on the street from exhaustion. Nobody else had seen this battle. Guedraut didn't even know it was happening until she heard them scream, "Kill the dog!"

I went to the iron gate and heard Guedraut asking her mother, "Why didn't you chase those boys away? That was no joke. Those were the same boys who almost drowned him. Didn't you hear about that?" I couldn't listen anymore. I needed to get up to my room. I had to drag myself on hands and knees because I was sore from the beating and exertion. Finally, I got to my bed and lay down.

A short while later, Guedraut came to my room and asked how I felt.

"Not so good right now, but I think I'll be OK after some rest." I found it hard to even talk, but I squeezed a few more words out. "Guedraut, thanks for everything you've done." Guedraut left. I undressed and went back to bed.

I got up the next morning, feeling much better. Although my muscles were strained and sore, my face had no scars from the night's battle. I found only a few black-and-blue spots on my hip.

After breakfast, Sossa sent me out to the field to rake up the wheat. I walked down the road with the big rake on my shoulder. The field was very near Joe and Rita's house, and they called out to me as I came near. They told me how badly I had beaten the Hitler Youth. They said the boys had black eyes and big bruises. One of them even had a broken shin and was on crutches.

"This is very bad news for you, Stanislaus," Rita told me. "They're going to lock you away!"

I took what Rita said very seriously. "This really is terrible news."

"It looks like we're not going to see each other anymore," Rita said unhappily. "I feel sorry for you – all the trouble you've gone through, so much trouble. But I believe you'll make it through all this. You'll make it."

Rita looked me straight in the eye. Then, I walked on to the field. I did my job and went home.

Saturday evening, the same Austrian officer from Schwarca came to take me to jail. I was there until Monday. They did this three weeks in a row. It was hard to spend Sundays behind bars while the sun was shining out. It really ate at me.

However, after that fight, the Hitler Youth didn't fight me or call me names anymore, even when I walked right past them. I was able to walk around our villages freely, day or night.

𝕾ix

═══THE FRENCH POW AND MAD WASYL═══

AFTER harvesting wheat, farmers had to thresh it to separate the grain from the chaff. In the villages around Sossa's, there was only one thresher, and all the farmers shared it.

The thresher was running at a neighbor's place when Guedraut and I went to help finish the job. This was a community effort. It took two strong men to carry the sacks filled with harvested wheat to the attic. After loading the hopper, one would come down with the empty sack and put it at the other end to be filled with the pure grain.

Everyone was sweating and very dusty from the bits of wheat husk rising in the air. From time to time, a woman would hand a ladle full of apple juice to the workers.

I was working with a Ukrainian named Wasyl. We had to take the wheat straw that had been separated from the grain away from the machine and dump it in the back of the barn. Wasyl had come to Germany voluntarily, and he was the meanest person I'd met so far. He was an informer, and he had a grudge against Poles. He was always growling, with an ugly demeanor. And he always picked on me!

At about 4 p.m., the machine was shut down while someone straightened out a problem. We took that opportunity to climb to the floor above us to find a spot to rest. We had climbed through an opening about ten feet above the ground floor and lay down on the straw. Wasyl seated himself closer to the opening. When I walked by him to go down to the toilet, he tripped me. I fell through the opening and hit my head on hay then I fell to the concrete.

A group of workers took me out of the barn unconscious and set me on a blanket. I awoke and saw blue sky, with no idea of what had happened. Beside me stood an old German man, Sossa's neighbor. He was rubbing me with his hand. In the background, I heard the machine running again. I sat up but couldn't get to my feet. My head was bent over, and I couldn't straighten my neck.

I asked the old German, "Why are you helping me? You saved my life."

"I lost two sons in the war, and I don't wish anyone else to die."

I thanked him and said I would always remember him. I felt so awful I thought I might die.

I heard the threshing machine stop and the workers heading into the house for a meal. The job was finished. The old man took me by the hand and helped me to the house. Everybody was sitting around a big table covered with a lavish spread of food and drink.

"Maybe you'll feel better if you eat or drink something," the old man said.

"Thanks, but I can't eat a thing. I'll take a glass of water, though.

The old man asked why I fell through the hole. I couldn't turn to face him because my neck was so stiff. I simply spoke, "Wasyl tripped me through the hole!"

"It seems like he wanted to kill you. Is he with us here?" the old man asked.

I figured he was, but I couldn't turn my head to look. So the old man turned my chair around and asked me to point out Wasyl, and I did. "There's the guy who tripped me."

Everybody looked at him, and Wasyl protested. "The boy just lost his balance and fell," he said.

The old man cut him off, though. "Wasyl, go outside! You have work to do."

He invited everybody else to stay, and then he said, "I think Stanislaus should be taken to the hospital as soon as possible. I think his injury is very, very bad. I don't know what'll happen if we don't get him some help."

A wagon filled with threshed wheat was to go into town soon. There was some concern that there'd be no place for me because it was so full, but there was a board sticking out of the wagon that I could sit on. People helped me out of the house and onto the board. I held on to both sides of the wagon. As we traveled, the man who was guiding the horses would look back from time to time to make sure I hadn't fallen off. He walked alongside the wagon and occasionally gave the horses the whip to keep them moving. He wanted to get me to the hospital as soon as possible.

We went to Dettelbach, a few kilometers from Schrcenau. We entered the gate at the hospital. The guide tied up the horses and put the brake on the wheels. He helped me into the hospital, and the sisters there took all my information. They took me to a room with two beds. When he saw that I was settled, the man with the wagon left.

A sister told me to take off my shirt and sit on the bed. She hung my shirt on a chair near the bed, picked up a wash bowl, and filled it with water. She washed my neck and torso. Then, she rubbed some kind of cream onto my back and began massaging it. Then, she put a robe on me and told me to lie down.

Later that evening, I met my roommate. He was a French officer and a prisoner of war. We both knew German, so we were able to talk to one another. He told me he'd been held in a German POW camp for two years. He said the food was good there. He'd had plenty to eat, and he also got packages from the Red Cross. Still, he got disgusted with being under guard day and night. So, he signed on for civilian labor. His status was like mine. He wasn't constantly guarded by men with rifles anymore.

He worked at the same brewery in Dettelbach where I picked up Sossa's beer, loading and unloading barrels. One day, a big barrel fell on his foot and broke a bone, and that put him in the hospital.

He told me his name was Maurice. We became good friends. He was trying to learn English, so he always carried a book of English lessons with him. He taught me some, and we began to speak English together. Every day, Maurice and I went outside to the garden, where we sat on a bench and practiced our English.

After a week in the hospital, my neck was still stiff and it hurt, even though the sister had massaged it from time to time.

Rita came by after I'd been in the hospital two weeks. She brought me a basket of apples and some good news. The Allies had taken the island of Sicily in August. I was very happy to hear the Germans had lost more ground. I got up and kissed Rita on the cheek.

Maurice saw me so happy and asked, "What's going on?"

As foreigners, we weren't supposed to know this news. I told him he must keep it a secret and then repeated the news Rita had told me. I introduced them to each other. I told Rita that Maurice had become a good friend, and I told Maurice about how Rita had lost her father on the Russian front about five months earlier. Rita couldn't stay very long. She asked how I felt and whether any of the Sossas had been to see me. "Not yet," I told her. She left soon afterward.

Sunday afternoon, Guedraut came. She brought homemade cookies. We talked for about twenty minutes. She was anxious to know when I'd be released. She told me she hated the farm life. She wanted to move to Wurzburg after the war and get married.

When she left, I started thinking just how kind she'd been to visit me. Rita and Guedraut had been my only visitors. After being exposed to so much cruelty, I wondered how these German women could be so understanding. They didn't look down on foreigners and were willing to visit them. War is created by men, not women, I thought. Certainly, this war was started by men.

Being in the hospital gave me the first long vacation from hard work in a long time. It was fun to visit the garden and view the beautiful profusion of flowers. It was fun to learn English with Maurice. I figured that language would be useful to me in the future. It was good to be in peaceful surroundings.

Despite the peace here, the thought of what Wasyl had done to me ate away at my soul. I wanted revenge badly. I tried to put these thoughts out of my mind over the two months I was in the hospital but was only partly successful.

Finally, at sunrise one Sunday, I thought over and over about Wasyl and what he'd done. These thoughts wouldn't leave me alone. Inside, something was pushing me to go to the village and kill Wasyl. "He has to pay for what he did to me," I thought. "I have to run away from the hospital while I'm still alive. ... My fall was no accident. He was trying to kill me. ... I have to get out of here and do what my heart tells me. ... I might be crippled the rest of my life. ... I'd better leave while I still have some strength, before my blood turns to water. ... I have to get him even if I'm sent to jail. What kind of life will I have anyway, if everybody feels free to pick on me? I'll be like a tree by the road, with everyone scraping the bark."

On and on, these thoughts tumbled through my head.

"This is your chance! You'll never have this chance again. It's still war time. One human's life is like a bubble on the water."

At eight o'clock, I got up and dressed myself. I stopped to look out the window at the morning sky, and then I looked at Maurice. My dear friend was asleep. I didn't wake him. I peeked out into the hall to see if anyone was around. Seeing no one, I walked out of the hospital without signing out.

It was cloudy and crisp as I started on the road to Schrcenau. My neck was bent so that I faced the ground. I picked up the pace when I got close to the village.

I began to think ahead. Wasyl was twenty-four. A short man, he was still stronger than I was. How was I going to do the deed I had in mind? A sharp stone in the road caught my eye. I picked it up and hefted it. With this weapon, I could kill Wasyl, I was sure.

I passed Sossa's and went straight to the neighbor's place where Wasyl worked. I opened the gate and saw Wasyl standing between the house and the barn in the back yard. He saw me coming. Not one word was said. When I got close enough, I started hitting him with the stone — on the head and over his ear. Wasyl seemed dizzy. Blood was running all over his shirt and the sidewalk. He tried to protect himself, but I attacked so furiously that he couldn't do much.

He ran to the kitchen and yelled for the lady of the house. She came out and began to scream, "What's happening here? What are you boys doing?"

"I'm going to kill him someday!" I shouted. "Look at me! I'm crippled. Look at how I'm suffering."

She saw that my neck was still bent so that I couldn't look up. I left then. I had carried an angry weight in my heart for two months, and I left it in the yard where I beat up Wasyl. "At least I spilled some of his blood on the sidewalk," I told myself. I didn't care what happened to me now.

When I walked into Sossa's kitchen, Guedraut heard me. "Is that you, Stanislaus? You're already out of the hospital? It's so good to have you back!" Then, she asked me how I felt.

"My neck is still stiff, but I feel better," I said. In my heart, I thanked God to be back at Sossa's. I went upstairs and dressed in my Sunday best. The rest of the day passed quickly, even though I spent most of it alone in my room.

The next day, the whole village was buzzing about how I beat up Wasyl, but no one reported me to Kessler. Maybe the lady who stopped our fight felt so bad for me that she didn't have the heart to turn me in. People were also talking about how I'd run away from the hospital. Somehow, I talked myself out of any trouble over it.

I never saw Wasyl or my friend Maurice again.

𝔖even

———————THE SOSSA FAMILY———————

WHILE I was in the hospital, Guedraut had confessed how much she disliked life on the farm, but she never showed it at home. She was good and cheerful most of the time. As the youngest child, she was the only one at home. Her three brothers, even the married one, were off to war, and her older sister lived in Wurzburg with her husband and kids.

Mrs. Sossa wasn't like Guedraut. She was very stuck up, and her personality was on the mean side. She made no move to help me when the Hitler Youth attacked me. In fact, she hardly talked to me for a year after I began working for them. However, when she warmed up to me, she spoke to me gently, and we even shared jokes.

Sossa himself, though, was another story. He never had a kind word for me. He hardly talked to me at all. He always looked angry, as though I had killed his sons. He was forever thinking and talking politics, and he was increasingly angry that the Germans were losing the war. He took that frustration out on me. He would jump right up to my face and, without warning, slap me. This happened all too regularly. I never hit back, but I put my hands up to protect my face. I knew I'd go to jail if I hit him. I'd had enough of that kind of trouble, so I tried hard to avoid it.

That was my main motivation at that point: "Don't get in anybody's way." My other guiding thought was to eat enough to build up my body. I wanted to regain the health I'd lost so far in this war, and I figured I'd need more strength in the future.

I'd finally made up a key to the cooler, and I'd made a key to the henhouse as well. If I was careful, I could get plenty of food and eggs. I still had my straw for the wine. I wouldn't take the food if I wasn't hungry. Sossa's stingy portions weren't enough for a growing boy, especially for one who needed to build up his muscles for strenuous work. Every day, I had to do my job and make sure I did it right. I didn't have any sick days. I had to get up and work, or Sossa might beat me or have me jailed. The only payment for my work was food, and Sossa wasn't giving me enough.

He never ran short of work, though. Sunday was the only day of rest. I had to feed and water the cows three times a day. With the early morning feeding, I wasn't allowed to sleep even an extra half-hour. In winter, I wasn't allowed to go into the house to warm up for a few minutes. From sunrise to sunset, cold or warm, snow or rain, six days a week, I wore the same work clothes. Nobody bought me a warm jacket for winter. My room wasn't heated, except for fifteen-minute periods at breakfast, lunch, and dinner. I shivered in bed at night. Thank God, I didn't get any worse problems than a bad cough.

In the fall, everything had to be harvested and picked up from the field so we could do our plowing. Every farm is constant work, of course.

Once, I was sent out to the property by the river to cut branches to make wicker baskets. I used a special knife for this job, cutting the branches, tying them up in bundles, and then piling the bundles together. When I was done with the cutting, I made a basket for Guedraut. I figured she could use it when we went to plant potatoes in the spring.

I brought the basket home and gave it to Guedraut.

"You made that, Stanislaus?" she said in surprise. "Oh, what a fine basket!"

Mrs. Sossa walked in as we were talking. Guedraut said, "Look at this beautiful basket Stanislaus made for me." That broke the ice with Mrs. Sossa. She was impressed with how well I had crafted the basket and the care I took in finishing it. She even showed it off to other villagers. Mrs. Sossa treated me well from that day forward.

When she came to milk the cows in the evening, she joked with me. "Do you have a girlfriend in the village?" She laughed. "Of course, you're going to stay with us after the war," she said with tongue in cheek. Another time, she asked if by any chance I came from a German family, because I had blond hair and blue eyes. She said that many Germans and Poles shared the same blood, but that some misunderstanding had caused trouble between them for hundreds of years.

As the end of 1943 approached, one of my chores was to cut the wood we'd use through winter. I used a hand saw and worked quickly. I cut piles upon piles of wood. I stacked the wood very neatly in front of the woodshed. Stacking the wood let it dry faster, but I had an ulterior motive for making these neat stacks. I wanted to shield myself from Sossa's watchful eyes.

Sossa would sit inside the warm house, sipping a glass of wine or smoking a cigar, and watch my every move from a window on the back yard. Without Sossa suspecting, I created my own wall of logs and left a peephole from which I could see more of the yard than Sossa could see from the window. With this barrier up, I could slow down some of the work. I could rest and even talk to Joe sometimes when he would come by with some bit of news about the war.

Because foreigners were denied access to radio and newspapers, I relied on Joe for word from the outside. Joe would tell me everything he heard about German losses: how many planes were lost, how many ships were sunk, how many Germans were killed, how many prisoners were taken, what ground they gave up.

One day, he told me how the Italian soldiers had thrown their rifles down and surrendered. They didn't want anything more to do with Hitler. We were all waiting for the end of the war, and for people caught in my situation, every German defeat meant that freedom was nearer.

I sawed wood for two months straight — every day until Christmas.

Everybody celebrated Christmas in Germany, but I didn't think the Germans did it as well as we did in

Poland, but then again, every country has its own customs. This was the first time I celebrated Christmas away from home. For those of us in forced labor, the holiday was sad. We weren't allowed to go to church. There was no holy bread broken for us, no one to wish us health and happiness, no one to talk to. I missed my family and longed for my church back home, where I could sing familiar Christmas hymns. I could imagine the Christmas tree decorated Polish style, hung with nuts, apples, candies, and cookies.

For Christmas, Alexander, one of Sossa's sons, came home on furlough. He was a high officer who'd been serving in Norway. Even so, he must have earned a medal for heroism to get a furlough at Christmas. Sossa was very happy to have his son home, even though the man was lazy and did nothing to help his father. Fathers love their sons, no matter what.

Alexander was very evil toward me. Any little slip-up was an excuse to beat me up. He wanted to cow me into doing more work. His motives were easy to read. I was very careful not to goof up while he was there. Fortunately, I hardly ever saw him. He slept until noon each day and never came out into the back yard.

Right after the holiday, we made schnapps. Now, this was an interesting job. Sossa arose at five o'clock and then woke me. He ordered me to bring water from across the street. He opened a barrel and started to fill buckets with fermenting apple wastes. I filled the still with water. Then, I had to get wood for the fire. I laid the wood alongside the still. Sossa carried the buckets of fermented apples and dumped them into the water in the still. He told me to go get more apple wastes from the barrel while he got a fire going under the still.

When I brought in the next bucket, the smell was so strong in the enclosed area that I felt dizzy, as if I'd had a couple of shots of schnapps already. I dumped my bucket into the boiling mixture in the still. When it was full of apple wastes, we put the top on the still and screwed it down.

Copper tubes ran out of the top and into gauges. As the still steamed, the schnapps began to drip through the copper tubing into a bucket. Sossa vigilantly monitored the gauges to check the alcohol content of the schnapps. When the bucket was full of schnapps, we set another one beneath the tube. We emptied the bucket into a fifty-liter bottle, the same kind used in office water coolers.

I kept feeding the fire and popped the lid every so often to stir the mixture. Now and again, Sossa would give me a shot of the schnapps. He tested it, too. For me, though, the best thing about this job was the chance to stay warm. Outside, it was cold and snow was on the ground.

When we finished making the schnapps, we had six fifty-liter bottles filled. We took them upstairs and put them away in the dance hall. I left, and Sossa locked the doors behind him. I got very little sleep that night. That sometimes happened after a very hard day.

One morning when Sossa got me up for work, I didn't get up right away. I was very sleepy, and it was still dark outside. I got up fifteen minutes later. When I got out back, Sossa grabbed me and screamed, "How many times do I have to go upstairs to get you down? You dog, you!"

I squirmed out of his grasp and said, "I'm here now. I'm here."

His son heard the commotion from upstairs and came running out in his pajamas. He came up to me and said, "Silence when my father talks to you! You dog!"

"All I said was, 'I'm here,' that's all."

"You say nothing! You have no right to say anything!" Then, he pounded me with his fist — six good shots. "If you do it again, I'll kill you, you dog!" For good measure, I guess, he hit me again in the nose. Blood started to run into my mouth and drip on my clothes. Fortunately, I'd put a hand up to protect my face and avoided a black eye. As hard as he hit, he might have knocked me out and I'd be lying on the concrete. I certainly didn't have the strength to fight a grown man who punched so hard, and I had to live with this man for another week.

The new year had started, and I wasn't very happy. How could I be happy with my face all bloody? I thought 1944 would begin much better than 1943. I was sure hoping I wouldn't be beaten again after all the abuse I'd taken in the last year. "Am I going to make it?" I asked myself. "Am I going to finish this road I'm walking, the road to safety? This road is so dangerous with all its twists and turns. Even if I don't want to walk it, I have to walk it to the end. There's no other road. Please, God, help me down the road to freedom."

Two weeks after Alexander's furlough ended and he shipped out to Norway, workers from Schrcenau — including all the Poles in town — were to cut wood in a forest about twenty-five kilometers away. The wood we cut would be divided among the villagers. Everybody had to get up very early for the trip. Guedraut got up before me to fix the coffee. She served me bread and butter for breakfast. She also packed me a brown-bag lunch, with a little bottle of schnapps inside.

At the corner, I met the workers I was to go with. There were twenty of us — Frenchmen, Poles, and some older Germans. We got aboard a trailer and sat on the benches screwed to its floor. A tractor pulled the trailer to the forest. It was very cold out, with about three inches of snow on the ground. The trailer was open to the wind and cold. We rode that way for twenty-five kilometers.

After passing through some small villages and big fields, we arrived at the forest. The old Germans started a fire so we could warm up. After we got warm, the Germans laid their coats on the ground by the fire. The work would keep the men warm, and the fire would keep the coats warm till the work was done. I didn't have a coat to put down there.

Hans, an older German neighbor of Sossa's, and I worked together well. He was pleased with the way I helped him split logs in two.

We began by chopping down tall trees. After we felled one, we'd cut it into four-foot lengths. We kept this up until we had cut a certain amount, and then we broke for lunch. We took the sandwiches from our bags and sat down to eat on a big log by the fire. Then, it was right back to work. Everybody did his best and worked as fast as he could. The four-foot logs were piling up.

When we got back home, it was already dark. Hans must have told Sossa how what a good worker I had been that day because the Sossas treated me like a king that night and gave me more to eat than usual. They told me to sit by the warm wood stove, and Guedraut brought me a little stool and a pan filled with warm water. She put some Epsom salts into the water and told me to sit down and soak my feet. I sat there almost an hour. Then, Guedraut asked if she should put more hot water into the pan. "Go ahead," I said. It felt good to be treated the way my family would have treated me.

The routine was the same for the next two days. Guedraut would wake me up, fix me breakfast, and pack my lunch, making sure I had that little bottle of schnapps. She'd look into my eyes and say, "Good luck! There's some schnapps to warm you up when you're out there." She had to sneak the schnapps to me. Thankfully, her parents were still asleep when she made my lunch. I brought the empty bottle home for a refill each night.

I didn't know how to repay Guedraut's kindness. All I was able to give her was a smile and words of thanks. As we rode out to the forest, I couldn't get Guedraut out of my mind. She was so kind to me. I wondered if she was feeling what I was feeling. I imagined her letting me kiss her. I didn't care what the Nazi law was. I wanted Guedraut. Then, I'd have to put these thoughts away as we arrived at the forest for work.

As we wrapped up the job, we took the branches that had been cut off the logs and put them in piles. These would be used for kindling. At lunch time that last day, we could hear Bamberg being bombarded. We heard the planes passing overhead. It was a cloudy day, but once in a while, you could see them as well. It was the first time I'd heard a German town being bombarded. The old Germans among us reacted in shock and anger. "Those are American planes! They're bombing our town! Those idiots! They're animals! They're dogs!"

The rest of us were happy. We Poles spoke excitedly to one another in our native tongue. I thought about my church in Rudnik and how it burned for days after the Germans bombed us. I thought about the bodies in the streets of Rudnik, killed by the German bombs. Finally, the time had come for the Nazis' towns to fall, just the way our towns fell in 1939. Now, these Germans would see what war meant. Now, we'd see if they really loved the war they started.

For weeks afterward, everyone talked about the bombing of Bamberg and of other towns and factories. Leipzig. Stuttgart. Schweinfurt. Braunschweid. The list went on. The bombings brought heavy losses to Germany. The villagers hung their heads now. The situation was very different. Reality was sinking in.

Sossa was mad as a dog about it. One morning, I just asked him what we were going to do that day, and he yelled, "Shut up, you dog!"

Then, the villagers stopped talking about the Allies' planes and the bombings. They just wondered what the spring would bring.

Sossa's married son brought his family to visit in April. He came in from Bamberg with his wife and small child. An army officer, he had used up most of his two-week furlough visiting his wife's family. So their visit to Sossa was quick. They pretty much just stopped by to say hello to his mom and dad. Then, they said goodbye and were on their way. Sossa, his wife, and Guedraut saw them off at the railroad station.

Later the same month, Sossa's other son, Andin, came home from the Russian front on furlough. He was a staff sergeant. He was different from his brothers, especially Alexander. He was understanding and didn't seem to have it in for me. He helped me with the work, and we'd talk about many subjects.

He asked about my family. "Do they write to you?"

He told me about what he went through on the Russian front. "The Russian front's not a toy to be played with," he said. I couldn't believe Andin was telling me, a foreigner, about the front.

Alexander didn't lift a hand to help around the place, and he hated me so much he wanted to skin me. Andin, on the other hand, helped me and told his dad to stay home and rest while he did the work.

Andin treated me like a younger brother. When the time came for him to return to the front, he even shook hands with me. "Goodbye, Stanislaus," he said. "It won't be very long before you'll get to see your family again."

"Goodbye, Andin. Return in peace, and God be with you."

No German serviceman had ever shaken my hand before, and I had never wished one a safe journey home, either.

Stan Domoradzki,
1943 Wartime II

Stan, Polish Guard
1945, Dachau

Stan, (middle), skiing in Garmisch, Germany won
first place in ski contest, 1945

River in Dachau
Stan, 1945

Inspection of Polish
Guard in Dachau.
Observed Polands
freedom May 3 parade,
1945

Left side-Stan
Dachau gate, 1945

Munich, 1945, German
SS headquarters. No
American headquarters.

Stan going to
USA, 1945

Polish Guards, 1945
Left - friend, Stan

Dachau - German
Nazi diving boards
for lake, 1945

Stan, Dachau
Train Station, 1945

First Infantry
Division, Mechanic
Motor Pool, Nurnberg
Furth, 1945

Stan, Polish Guard by
horse barn in Dachau,
1945

Stan, Army, USA
uniform, 1945

Stan, Alabama unit,
Munich, Germany 1945

Olympia Dominiak, she
was Polish, from
Siberia. Stan married
her in 1950

€ight

BOMBER CRASH

THE summer of 1944 came, warm and dry. I hadn't been so happy in quite some time. The Allies' bombing runs made me feel that my freedom was at hand. I sang and whistled as I worked, for I saw a new world ahead of me.

At first, the Allies bombed our region only by night. Planes launched flares to make their targets visible. These flares made the landscape bright as day. Within weeks, the bombers came day and night, every few hours.

The first time I saw an Allied bomber squadron, the four-engine planes glinted in the sun. The villagers raised their heads to look up at them. The bombers were many and they flew very high. They sounded like a swarm of bees. It was music to my ears. The bombs they carried meant freedom for prisoners in the concentration camps and jails, as well as the foreigners like me, who were working as slaves.

On the ground, life was still hell, but in the air, you heard the sound of freedom.

I heard the German villagers talk about how Monte Cassino had fallen when the Polish Second Corps under British command stormed the old Italian monastery on May 18. Taking the monastery was an important step in breaking the Gustav Line, the Germans' strong line of defense in the Italian mountains. Situated atop a mountain, Monte Cassino gave the Germans a good position to hold off their enemies, and they fortified that advantage with great numbers of artillery and pillboxes. Soldiers from around the world — the United States, Britain, India, France, Algeria, Morocco, and other countries — fought bitterly in four battles over the first five months of the year to pry this fortress from German hands, for it blocked the way to Rome. On June 4, soon after Monte Cassino was taken, Rome became the first Axis capital to fall.

The Polish Second Corps was formed in Siberia. Stalin had shipped Polish prisoners to Siberia, but when the Germans invaded Russia in 1941, he freed the Poles and enlisted them to fight the Nazis. In 1942, Stalin agreed to transfer the corps to British command. In 1943, they trained in Iraq, which was then held by the British, and were shipped to Italy at the end of the year. Nearly 3,800 Poles died in the battle to take the monastery.

On June 6, 1944, Joe told me that the Allies were invading France at Normandy. Paratroopers were still landing. I thanked him for the news, happier than ever because I felt that the Allies were in my back yard.

Then, the most unbelievable news came. On July 20, a group of Hitler's own officers had planted a bomb under a conference table in an effort to kill him. The bomb went off, but Hitler was not killed. We heard that his right hand was paralyzed.

At about the same time, the Soviets drove the Germans out of Russia and began to push them back through Poland. On August 1, as the Red Army neared Warsaw, the Polish resistance began to riot against the Germans. The resistance wanted to liberate the city before the Soviets did. The resistance members knew Stalin's occupation would be as bad as Hitler's. The Germans killed tens of thousands in the next few months. They left nothing standing in Warsaw. Poles left alive in Warsaw were sent into forced labor or concentration camps.

Such resistance to the Germans was rising everywhere in occupied Europe. After three years of fighting, the Yugoslav resistance chased the Germans out in 1944. These uprisings, I believed, would make the war end sooner.

Meanwhile, the Allied bombing continued. Sometimes when I slept, the bombing raids would wake me, and I'd go to the window to watch the planes.

The Nazis set up a hidden airport near our village. There was no time to build a proper runway, so the planes took off from the highway. The planes were hidden among the trees and covered with branches. When Allied planes were in the vicinity, three or four of these hidden planes would take off after them.

Allied fighters shot them down almost as soon as they got into the air. I saw many dogfights too, and the

Germans usually got the worst of them. The Allies suffered losses, too. Once, I saw parachutists escaping a plane shot down by German pilots. However, the Allies clearly were overpowering the Luftwaffe.

The Allies sent fighter planes in to scout the terrain, looking for targets. They could spot anything. One found the airport hidden near us and destroyed it before the planes could get off the ground.

The fighters would attack anything. They'd hit trains and railroad stations, any wheeled vehicle. They'd even attack tractors, buses and bicycles sometimes. The fighters' bullets set many vehicles aflame.

These fighter planes also carried small bombs. When the first fighters to fly over jettisoned their empty reserve fuel tanks, the villagers thought they were unexploded bombs, avoiding them for fear they would go off. Somehow, the villagers found out these were just fuel tanks. People then took the tanks home and used them. Some were lucky enough to find fuel left in the tanks.

After a particularly heavy raid nearby, Nazi commanders ordered the villagers to organize Volkssturm (people's army) units, under Joseph Goebbels' plans for total mobilization of the German population as the war came to Germany. These groups of civilians armed themselves with shotguns, pistols, or whatever other weapons they had at home. Their mission was to patrol the fields and roads after bombing raids, looking for downed Allied airmen. A group of twenty men went out every day from Schrcenau.

Villagers said that the Volkssturm shot many of the airmen, but that they also turned others over to the

Nazi police. Kessler and the mayor shot four parachutists themselves. I would hear much of this talk as I went about Sossa's business. The villages were buzzing with all this news.

A munitions factory near Schweinfurt came under a daily bombardment. The Germans typically rebuilt such facilities, but this incessant attack gave them no chance to do so.

With the fighters and bombers, life was becoming more and more dangerous on German soil. It became almost impossible to go out in daylight. Motorists had to listen for approaching planes. Army trucks, buses, and cars traveled with one person on the hood who'd shout a warning at the sound of an Allied plane. The driver would stop immediately, and everyone would hit the dirt, waiting for an attack.

Some fighters came in so low, no one could see them, and even the men on the hoods wouldn't hear them in time, dooming the vehicles on the ground. These attacks could come at any time and any place, even on the gravel roads, and they were increasing in number.

The Nazis were working on the atom bomb. Fortunately, they were months away from finishing when the Allied forces ended the project. Still, the Germans tried anything and everything to win the war. Hitler's scientists developed missiles — the V-1 and the V-2 — that rained tons of explosives on England, beginning in June. The British suffered heavy civilian casualties. Yet, the Allies kept pushing into Germany. They intended to push all the way to Berlin.

The Allied war effort completely disrupted Germany. Nothing was operating anymore. The railroads and factories were bombed out. The Germans couldn't produce ammunition or gasoline. They couldn't keep up with repairs.

German civilians were abandoning the cities for rural villages and towns as fast as possible. Air-raid sirens sounded every day. The bombers kept coming and coming. At night, I couldn't sleep. Every time I'd lie down, it seemed, the sirens went off and the planes buzzed overhead.

One night, Guedraut came right up to my bed and said, "Get up! Get up if you want to stay alive! Don't you hear the noise outside?" I went downstairs with her very quickly. Then, we heard a big blast and felt the ground shake like an earthquake. The whole area was lit up by flares. I didn't sleep anymore that night. The villagers were walking the streets and talking about how bad this bombardment looked. To me, it looked like the world was ending from midnight till six.

Sometime after 5 a.m., I heard an explosion in the air. Pieces of a plane rained down on Schrcenau, landing on streets and roofs. The whole plane fell apart, everyone aboard blown to bits.

The high command from Kitzingen, Kessler, the mayor, and the Volkssturm went out to the site where the largest part of the wreckage had fallen. They trained a light on the area and saw that it was a four-engine bomber, flesh and bone were strewn among the pieces of the plane.

They wouldn't let us Polish people close to the crash. I wanted to see, though, so I went through the back yard. I leaned against a neighbor's hay barn and peeked out. There was no one around, so I crawled closer to the crash site. I was shocked and scared, but I looked at the engines and chunks of metal that were scattered on the ground. Some of the pieces were blackened by the explosion. I also saw fingers, legs, and heads strewn among the metal about ten to twenty yards away from me. The main body of the plane dug a deep furrow in Kessler's field as it crashed. A man's body lay about a yard from the Catholic cemetery. I thought darkly that he'd almost landed in the right place.

"My God, you came so far to bring us freedom, and now you're dead," I thought. I got down on my knees, made the sign of the cross and prayed for their souls. Then, I went home.

German authorities combing the area found the remains of seven men. These bombers had nine-man crews, but the authorities couldn't find enough pieces to account for the other two. When I heard about this, I wondered if they'd been able to parachute out. Maybe they were hiding in the forest, or maybe their bodies had been hurled away from the crash site by the explosion.

The high command and some special officers discussed where the remains should be buried — in the cemetery or with the dogs? The villagers voted to bury them in the cemetery. However, the Nazis ordered that the grave go unmarked. The bodies were interred in a corner near the fence where the one airman's body fell.

On Sunday, Germans from nearby villages came to the crash site. People came by bicycle, on horseback, in cars, and on motorcycles. Many people were there.

The crippled soldiers from the hospital in Schwarca came. Prisoners came. Even we foreigners were able to go.

A group of Polish people from Schrcenau went to the airmen's grave and placed a small, wooden cross and many flowers atop it.

When Kessler and the mayor heard about it, they hurried to the grave. They threw away the cross and the flowers.

The mayor then put an angry question to the crowd.

"Who put the flowers and the cross on this grave?"

No one answered.

"I don't want to see any more crosses or flowers here. They are dogs! They got what they asked for! They don't deserve a marker! If this happens again, I'll have someone shot! Let this be a warning to all of you!"

Nine

---CHILD IN RUBBLE---

A squadron of planes attacked Kitzingen at noon on a very clear day. I was working in Sossa's back yard as the bombers and escort planes flew overhead. I threw down my tools and watched. I heard the air-raid siren in Kitzingen, and the sound unnerved me. Still, I kept watching the planes and counting them. Then, I saw bombs shining bright in the sun as they fell on Kitzingen. I felt that each explosion was bringing me closer and closer to freedom. Out on the street, groups of German women stood weeping. Kitzingen was their neighbor. Many of them had relatives there.

The next day, a group of foreigners was pressed into duty to help residents of Kitzingen dig victims and survivors out of the rubble. We left Schrcenau with a group of older Germans aboard a trailer pulled by a tractor, just as we had gone to the forest to cut wood that winter.

In Kitzingen, I was ordered to dig out the rubble covering a cellar. I had no sooner started swinging my pick than the air-raid siren sounded its terrible blast again. Everybody knew they had to get out of town because there was no safe cover in Kitzingen. As I ran out of town, I saw bodies on the streets, sidewalks and stairways waiting to be picked up by truck and taken out of the city. The bombs were already falling and exploding before we made it out of town. Fortunately, I got out without a scratch.

Outside of town, a crowd of people milled in a meadow. When I got a bit closer, I could see that the meadow was filled with the dead. People tearfully tried to identify the bodies by the clothes they were wearing. Crying could be heard some distance off.

The reality of war finally visited these Germans. Now, they saw the same destruction their armies had rained on others. Their tears fell like never before.

After fifteen minutes, the all-clear sounded. Slowly, everybody returned to the job of digging people out. I stuck with a Russian named Mike, who, like me, worked in Schrcenau. Although he was three years older, he was shorter than I was. There were no guards watching us, no one pointing rifles at us as we walked back to work.

In our path stood a large pile of rubble and a fallen building. Most of the workers went to the left to get past it. Mike and I went to the right and entered a narrow street. Then, we heard a very faint sound somewhere in the rubble. It sounded as though it was coming from a cellar.

I asked Mike, "Do you hear something? I hear something like a baby crying."

"I hear it, too," Mike said.

We looked for a window or other entrance to the cellar. We found a window on the far side, but we had to pull away a pile of bricks and other debris to get in. The crying had stopped. Then, we saw that the window had steel bars on it. Fortunately, the bricks around the window had been shaken loose, and we were able rip the bars out of the frame. We broke out the glass and entered the cellar. I went in first. Mike was scared. "I'll follow right after you," he said.

In the cellar, the only light came from the window we'd broken. Half the cellar was in ruins, and the wall looked to be in dangerous shape. We walked over joists, plaster, and boards, looking for whomever had been crying. No one was crying now.

Mike said, "Whoever it was might be dead, or maybe they ran away!"

"Maybe we just imagined we heard something," I said.

Because we couldn't see or hear anyone, we made up our minds to leave. As we were going, we noticed some wine barrels and decided to get a drink before we left. We were very thirsty from our work. We knocked on one barrel and heard the sloshing of some wine. We tried the spigots, but they were locked.

Mike asked, "What are we going to do?"

"Nothing. I've already had experience with locked barrels," I said. I surveyed the basement for some kind of tool that would let us get at the wine. I spotted a very thin inner tube from a bicycle. I grabbed it and said, "I have to cut the tube into pieces, but I need something to cut it. The only way to get at the wine is to pop the corks on top of the barrels and suck through this."

Mike found a shard of glass, and we cut the tube into two equal pieces.

I looked around the cellar again. Pieces of a stairway, broken rubble, a door covered with all junk. I saw something else that would have made it easier to get at the wine and called to Mike to tell him. Then a child started wailing. I froze in my tracks. In a wary voice, Mike asked, "Who's that?" and came toward me.

"I don't know. The sound came from that dark corner."

We moved toward the sound. I looked up at the caved-in ceiling. Then, I spotted a small child, a girl. She had her hands against the wall. I touched Mike and pointed toward her. "There's a little girl." She had stopped crying. She was pointing toward the broken stairs.

"There's my mama," she said.

I didn't know what to tell her. The situation was very clear. The spot where the little girl was pointing was covered with rubble and heavy joists. There was no way anyone trapped under that could be alive. Her mama was dead and buried under the rubble.

I choked up, and Mike didn't know what to say. I edged closer to her and took her hand. "Come over here. Don't be afraid." She came with us to the window. In that light, we could see she was about five years old. She was dressed in a short, ruffled dress. She had short, blond hair that was slightly curly on top, and she was dirty from the rubble. She seemed to be all out of tears. She repeated, "There's my mama," and pointed at the same spot. "Open the door for my mama so she can get me something to drink. I'm thirsty."

Mike said, "What are we going to do with her?"

"There's no water, but she wants something to drink."

"Let's give her a little bit of wine," he said.

He quickly got on the barrel and began to drink. The girl was still motioning to where her mother had been. How could I explain to her? I said, "Mama is on the other side of the rubble. As soon as we get out of here, we'll go over there to find your mama, but now you have to go to the barrel and get some wine."

She saw what Mike was doing, so we had no trouble getting her to drink. Mike held the tube, and I showed her how to suck on it, getting myself a little drink in the process. I held her up and gave the tube to her, and she drank her fill. Then, I put her down.

"Leave her alone for a while," Mike said. "We have to have some more wine. It's very good."

When we were done, we put the girl up on the barrel and gave her a little more wine. The girl was sweet and trusting and was very happy to be with us. When she finished, she had a little wine on her chin and her dress.

"Well, let's have another sip," Mike said, "but we'd better not give her any more."

"You're right. We don't want to get her dizzy."

As we moved toward the window to leave, the air-raid siren sounded again. Moments later, we heard a blast and saw the building across from us crumble. Some bricks fell through the window, and our exit was blocked with rubble, making it suddenly very dark in the cellar. The little girl screamed in terror. Mike and I were also scared, but we did our best to comfort and quiet her.

When we calmed her down, the cellar became very quiet. As far as we knew, that was our only exit. "What are we going to do?" we asked each other. We looked all around us in the darkness for some way out, but it was hard to see.

"We're not going to get out of here," Mike said. "We're done for, all three of us." He said it loudly, on the edge of panic. Then, he screamed for help.

"Calm down!" I said. "We've got to think and look for a hole to the outside."

After a moment, Mike said, "You're right. Let's look."

I noticed a pinpoint of light in one corner. "Mike, come over here a minute and take a look. Do you see that light? What do you think?"

"It looks good to me," Mike said. "Let's try to dig it out."

"Yes. Let's do it."

We tried to reach the little hole, but it was too high. We had to climb up on some rubble before we could begin to dig out, using some two-by-fours we found in the rubble. The little hole got bigger and bigger. After some hours of work, we were finally able to peer out at the blue sky again. We couldn't reach the opening to pull ourselves out, but now that there was some good light, we found some planks and improvised a scaffold. Mike climbed onto the board and wormed his way through the hole. I handed the little girl to him, and I was the last to climb out.

On the street, we each took one of the little girl's hands in ours. We tried to talk to her and asked her her name. She didn't answer, but she looked very happy to be out of the cellar. We were happy, too.

As we walked down the street, we passed more rubble. The sun was low in the sky. Ahead of us, we spotted a group of German workers.

"What are we going to do?" Mike said. "We have to make a decision fast."

"We can't tell them we were in the cellar and drank wine all day," I said. "And the Germans won't believe us if we tell them we found the little girl in the cellar. If we tell them the truth, they're going to drag their questions out till tomorrow morning."

"So what should we do?"

"We'll turn the girl over to these Germans and say we found her wandering around on the street lost," I said. "Then, we'll head over to our group, if they haven't left yet."

The Germans bought my story and asked no questions. They didn't say thank you, either. We were happy, though, not to have to worry about the girl anymore. Now, the Germans could worry about her.

When we reached our group, they were packing up their tools, getting ready to leave. "Where were you all day?" the group leader asked. "We were just wondering about you guys. I thought you were killed."

"We were very close to death," I answered. "We're here now, though. When we started to come back after the air raid, a group of Germans gave us some work to do. They kept us busy until they started packing to go. So we came back here."

"How many bodies did you find?" he asked.

"None," we said. There were no more questions.

Sitting in the trailer, everybody talked about the bodies and other things they dug out of the rubble. The next day, the same group headed to Kitzingen on the same grim task. When Mike and I arrived, ready to go, they wouldn't take us. I guess they figured we'd been useless the day before and would be of no help again.

Instead, I was very happy to set out with Guedraut and Sossa to harvest potatoes. Mike went on to his place. We never told anyone in Schrcenau about the little girl. We never heard anymore about her, but I believe she was in good hands. The Germans would took good care of her.

Ten

CHESS IN JAIL

IT was a cloudy, mid-September day in 1944, and Sossa decided it was a perfect time to plow. "Hitch up the cows and ready the wagon," he told me. When I was done, we rode out to Sossa's field. We unloaded the plow and hitched the cows to it.

"I'm going to plow it by myself," Sossa said. "You pick up the rocks in my path."

The ground was turning over nicely for him, but then he plowed too close to the iron bar marking the boundary of his field. The plow blade hit the bar and bent.

First, he swore at the cows, then he cursed me. His language was very foul. I was close by and said, "I didn't do anything, so don't cuss at me. Don't blame me."

Sossa reacted violently, jumping away from the plow and coming toward me. Then, he shook me and said sternly, "Just shut your mouth, you dog!"

I turned away but couldn't resist gesturing in protest. Sossa saw red and grabbed a hook from the ground near the wagon. He came after me. Out of the corner of my eye, I saw him swinging the hook at me. I grabbed the hook as he swung it downward and blunted its impact on my head. I wrestled the hook away from him as blood rushed from my head onto my face and neck. Sossa lost his balance after I pulled the hook away and fell in furrow.

I took a step back. In the distance, I saw Kestner, another farmer from the village. He had been riding his wagon to a nearby field and saw the whole incident. He grabbed a fork off his wagon and came running to Sossa's aid. He jabbed me with the fork. I knew I couldn't fight both of them, so I ran. As I was getting away, I saw the other farmer helping Sossa up. "They'd have killed me for sure if I stayed," I told myself.

When I was far enough away that they couldn't see me anymore, I started walking back to Sossa's house. I took a shortcut through the fields — past potatoes, beets, clover, grass, and fruit trees. I held a handkerchief to my head to try to stop the bleeding. I didn't know what I was going to do with myself. The war wasn't over yet, and here I was, in trouble with a German farmer. I got to the back yard, and thought, "The police will come for me for sure." I sat in the yard about a half an hour, then I went to the garden. I saw the apples were ripe for the picking and took a couple. They were delicious.

By now, the blood had stopped flowing. It matted my hair and dried on my shoulders. I went from the garden to Sossa's back yard. I was almost to the house when Guedraut spotted me. "What happened?"

I took a deep breath. "Your dad tried to kill me!"

Guedraut said nothing but rushed into the kitchen. By this time, Sossa was on his way back from the field. He walked up and saw me in the back yard but didn't say anything. They called me into the house for lunch as if nothing had happened.

Things went well the rest of the week, so by the weekend, I had almost forgotten the incident. I was reminded Saturday night when the Austrian policeman rode his bicycle up to Sossa's house and took me off to jail. In the morning, the officer gave me breakfast. Then, he took me out back and ordered me to clean his motorcycle. I liked being out in the sunshine so much that I did a good job for him.

He called me in for lunch. I ate and then he told me to come sit by his desk. "Stanislaus, you should watch your tongue and be more careful! I see dark times coming for you. You're on the road to a concentration camp if you don't watch out. I'll try to protect you. I'm not a German. I'm originally from Austria," he said, leaving unsaid that he sympathized with my plight.

"I promise. I'll be more careful."

"I'm going to try hard to work things out for you. Tomorrow morning you will be taken to Kessler's farm. You'll be working hard for him. He's a tough disciplinarian. I understand you very well, Stanislaus. I understand your situation, but this is the best I can do for you now. As you know, Kessler and the mayor have clout because they're Nazis."

He looked at me and then at the chessboard on his desk. I followed his gaze, and then he turned his back. That's when I moved the black knight. He was playing

136

white. When he turned around and saw my move, he moved a pawn to defend.

"I'll take white, and you take black," he said. "Let's start over because white moves first."

So we started to play. I took some of his pieces, but he didn't get any of mine. Then he advanced his knight. "What will be, will be," he said. "You live once; you die once." I hadn't realized he was playing intently. He smiled and took my knight with his queen.

Then, I moved and took his queen.

"Well, it looks like you know how to play chess!" he said. We had decided to have another game when someone knocked on the door. He told me to go to the cell in the basement.

On Monday morning, the officer took me to Sossa's to pick up my belongings. When I came down, we went straight to Kessler's, and the old thug put me right to work. Kessler had four other foreign workers to tend his five hundred acres. They were Amelia from Krakow and Olga from Kiev. Then there was Amelia's relative, Johann, also from Krakow, and Joseph from Dembica. Kessler worked us all hard because we were few in number for such a big farm.

Kessler kept cows, horses, pigs, chickens, ducks, and geese. He had tractors for field work, and in the winter, he cut wood with a belt-driven splitter that attached to the tractor. He had a wheat harvester and just about any other machinery a farm could use. With all that machinery, we still had to work hard, by hand, in the fields. We sweat in the sun all day long.

Nothing was good enough for Kessler. I was the new worker, and I knew I had to watch my every step. Still, he came into the field and beat me in front of the others for no reason at all. This rattled everybody.

When Kessler left the field, Amelia told me, "I don't know how you're going to get through this. We've been beaten by Kessler, too, but it wasn't as bad as you got. He really worked you over. Who knows what'll happen tomorrow?"

I didn't answer. I was scared. From what I'd seen of the workers on Kessler's farm, they were being destroyed slowly. The girls' legs were crooked, and they had back pain from carrying the big cans of milk to the street. In the morning, the girls had to get the milk ready, clean the filters, and put the milk cans out for pickup. It was a strenuous job. One of Kessler's former workers, a Russian named Ivan, had two ruptures, and Kessler would not take him to the hospital. He just told Ivan to work harder.

There were also rumors that he had beaten some of the French and Polish prisoners of war who worked for him so savagely that he crippled them. Then, he sent them to other towns, maybe even to concentration camps.

One person Kessler didn't bother too much was Joseph. He worked with the horses — cleaning and feeding them — as well as in the field. Joseph was a big man and kept himself in good condition, so Kessler might have been afraid of him. If Joseph turned on Kessler, the Nazi's only defense would be to shoot the big man.

In the evening, we had to milk and feed the cows after coming in from the field. Then, we had a dinner of potatoes and salad with vinegar. When we were done for the night, we got together in our sleeping quarters and talked — even the girls. We had separate quarters from the girls, who had rooms in Kessler's house. Our four rooms were clean, but the rest of the building needed painting.

Amelia and I became good friends. One Sunday, we headed out to another village for a dance. At about two in the afternoon, after we'd reported to the mayor, we began walking and talking. We crossed the bridge and then walked down by the trail near the river. We came across a spot near the river where the bushes were thick and the grass was soft. We sat down and talked some more. Then, hidden away in the bushes, we had sex.

Later, we continued our interrupted journey to the dance hall. A Polish band was playing and doing very well. Sometimes, the SS closed the dance hall, saying, "Our soldiers at the front don't dance or listen to music, so why should you?" But that Sunday wasn't one of those times. Amelia and I danced into the night.

Eleven

GUEDRAUT

WHEN I was sent to Kessler's farm, Wasyl was sent to Sossa's. Guedraut hated Wasyl. She said he was a sloppy, dirty man. She tried very hard to get me back.

Remember that Sossa's also was the post office. Guedraut used to get the mail and deliver it in the nearby villages, riding her bike with her dog running alongside for protection. This made her familiar to everyone. She was very well liked and had some pull among the people, so she was certain she would get me back to Sossa's farm.

She pleaded my case around town, saying it was no good for me to work for Kessler. She told people I was a nice young man. She told them how clean I kept my room and the yard. She told them how I brushed the cows. (I always followed the advice of my teacher back in Poland, who said, "Keep yourself clean, that means health.")

Guedraut even got her parents to agree to take me back.

140

Kessler owned a lot of property. His buildings, cow stalls, and hay barns were all very big. His back yard, though, was a mess. The smell was terrible, even from a distance. Kessler worked everyone much harder than Sossa did, but Sossa was only a small farmer. All of Kessler's workers complained about their health and the way he treated them. That's just the way he wanted it. If his workers died, he didn't care. He'd just get more. The girls working at Kessler's farm were young, in their twenties. But everyone at his farm looked older than their years.

So I was glad, after eleven days of hard labor and beatings at Kessler's, when Guedraut got her way. She walked me out of Kessler's stinky place. In the bargain, she got rid of Wasyl, who was returned to Kessler's farm, where he could be messy. From then on, any time I passed Kessler's I just held my nose and walked as fast as possible.

I liked Guedraut very much and was very grateful for what she had done for me. I could tell that she liked me, too. We worked together like a team. We did everything together, even the laundry. Guedraut hated washing her father's handkerchiefs, dirty as they were from the snuff he used to blow into them, so I offered to wash them for her. I didn't mind. I'd do anything to help Guedraut.

In the laundry room, there was big tub in which we made whiskey. It doubled as a bath tub for Guedraut. I'd haul water from the pump across the street to fill the tub. Then, I'd put wood under it and start a fire to warm the water. When it was good and warm, I'd snuff the fire. Then, Guedraut would get her towel and soap from the house and lock herself in for a private bath.

One day after lunch, I prepared the wagon so we could pick up some beets. The wagon had to be boarded up on all sides, so it looked like a big box, to keep the beets from tumbling out. They would be winter feed for the cows. I hitched the cows to the wagon, and Guedraut came out of the house carrying a bottle of water for us.

Guedraut sat in the bottom of the wagon as I climbed up on the front seat to guide the cows. We were heading toward the bridge, when we took the left turn onto the gravel road that followed the Main to the beet field. The day was mild and sunny. Guedraut wore what they called a house dress, which was comfortable for work. (In those days, women always wore dresses.) Only her head showed above the sides of the box on the wagon.

Guedraut had her legs up and apart with her dress down to her hips. She didn't have any underpants on. As I guided the cows, I'd glance back toward the bridge and get a quick look at her, too. Then, I'd look back at the tower and glance again at her.

We were on the gravel road approaching the hill where we picked up rocks that we used to repair roads. I was still taking those peeks at the bridge and her legs. All of a sudden, the rope I used to guide the cows got loose, and I lost my balance. I tumbled back into the wagon on top of Guedraut. I tried to get up, feeling embarrassed. Something told me not to be in too much of a hurry. That same something told me to kiss her. I did, and then I kissed her again and played with her breasts.

She said, "Don't be afraid, Stanislaus." Then, she kissed me back. "Look to see if anyone's around."

She lay down in the wagon as I scanned the land-scape. All I saw was the road, the sky, and the cows still pulling the wagon toward the beet field. "There's nobody out there."

"I know what you're after," she said as if she didn't have a part in it, "but it's dangerous. You know if they catch us, they might shoot us or put us in jail."

"There's just the two of us here, and neither one of us is going to tell anyone," I answered.

Guedraut hugged and kissed me, and we had sex. For me, it was the first time with a beautiful German girl. It was on my mind for a long time.

The cows had already reached the beet field and had stopped before a pile of them. Feeling good, Guedraut and I got to work loading the beets into the wagon. We finished quickly. Then, we rode past the house, up the hill to the root cellar, about a mile from the field. The cellar was carved out of a cave in a little hill. The pad-locked door, almost hidden by the surrounding brush, peeked out at the gravel road. It was hidden so well that a casual passerby would never notice it. It could easily be used as a bomb shelter. The cellar floor was a few steps down from the surface. To let air in, holes — just big enough for someone to crawl through — were carved out of the walls. We would pack these with straw in the winter to insulate the cave from bitter cold. It was always dark in there unless the door was open wide. On cloudy days, we lit candles to see. The root cellar held our stores of potatoes, carrots, the red beets people ate, and the white beets we fed to the cows.

The weather got cooler as we unloaded the beets. When we finished, we went home. Guedraut and I didn't have sex on our minds anymore. There was too much work to do, and we were scared to take the risk again.

At about that same time, Guedraut's older sister, Katy, and her family came from Wurzburg. Their house had been damaged when the Allies bombed the city, so they moved in with Sossa — Katy; her husband, Emil; their seven-year-old son, Emil Jr.; and their five-year-old daughter, Hilda. Emil was a top engineer at a plant in Wurzburg. He continued to work there, staying at Sossa's only on the weekends. He was an understanding man, who never swore at me or hit me. He always treated me like a human being.

In addition, two shepherds came to stay at Sossa's. They had an agreement with the farmer that their sheep could graze on Sossa's field. The sheep, in turn, fertilized it. Still, they paid Sossa room and board. The two men slept upstairs close to my room. One of them was German. He was a good-looking, strong man, who limped. I think he faked the limp to get out of the army because I saw him a few times when he thought no one was looking and he wasn't limping. The other one was Polish. They had three dogs that helped them herd the sheep. At the end of the day, they'd arrive with one dog tied to their wagon. The other two stayed with the sheep at night.

Winter days are short, but for us, workdays were still long. The tavern was open longer hours, usually from noon to about 11 p.m. or midnight. Imagine how much Guedraut had to work.

Every weekend there was a meeting in the tavern that lasted late into the night. The mayor and Kessler

144

always came for the meeting. As I was sleeping one night after one of those meetings, I heard someone open the door to my room and walk in. "Stanislaus," he called. I knew the voice. It was that thug Kessler.

"The killer's here," I thought. He pounced on me, striking three quick blows to my face with his ham-sized fist. I don't know why he hit me, but as quickly as he struck, he was gone. My face was hot and it hurt. When I put the light on, I saw my nose was bleeding and my pillow was full of blood. I put my head back to stop the flow.

"Why did he do this to me?"

The next day I was still wondering why he did it. I told myself, "I have to get even with him somehow after the war. I've had enough of this. I'd kill him if I had the chance." I swore death to Wasyl, Alexander and the Hitler Youth. "I'd like to slap Sossa's face, too. I'm going to get even with the people who made me bleed on sidewalks and beds, fields and wood piles."

I couldn't be angry at Guedraut, though. I asked her that day if she could find out why Kessler beat me. She found out that her dad had asked Kessler to do it. She felt bad about what her father did. I had nothing against Guedraut. We never argued or spoke a mean word to each other.

Sossa wouldn't let me put food on my plate for fear I'd take too much. Sossa told Guedraut to serve me and to put only so much on the plate. She did that for me — breakfast, lunch, and dinner. Guedraut was my friend the whole time I worked for Sossa.

Twelve

AMERICAN PILOTS

MY second Christmas in Germany passed quietly. The winter was milder than the year before, and the calendar page turned to 1945. The bombardment in our area stopped, at least for a little while, but we could still see and hear the bombers. They flew over us on their way to cities like Berlin. We knew they had a tough job ahead of them.

In the daytime, they flew very high, contrails streaming white behind them in the blue sky. To me, it sure looked good. At night, the sound of their engines told us they were flying over. To me, their sound was like a song. I spent many nights wrapped in a feather quilt by the open window listening to the beautiful chorus of the airplanes. The Allies touched my heart because they were bringing us all closer to freedom. I know I wasn't alone in that feeling. Millions were counting the minutes, hours, and days.

One mid-February day, the snow had melted, the sky was clear, and a light wind was blowing. Sossa told me to take the wagon to the root cellar and pick up some beets. In the coldest parts of December and January, we didn't go out there because we had loaded the cellar by the hay barn with most of our supplies. As spring approached, it was time to replenish those stocks.

I had to take the wagon past the cellar's big arched door and then back up to it. I put the brake on the wagon, unlocked the door, put the key in my pocket, opened the creaky door wide, and walked in. I very seldom lit a candle. The door gave me all the light I'd need. I set the basket I'd use to carry out the beets in the middle of the floor.

Suddenly, someone grabbed me from behind, hands around my neck, almost choking me. A second man, with a beard and a fur-lined leather jacket, stuck a very cold, 45-caliber pistol to my head.

"You Kraut," he said.

I could hardly breathe because of the choke hold, let alone speak. Finally, I managed to squeeze some words out in broken English. "Me Polish, me Polish! Me no Kraut." My captor relaxed his grip, and the pistol went down. I took a look at the man who had held me. He, too, had a beard and wore a fur-lined leather jacket. I noticed a patch on the side of the jacket emblazoned with an eagle and realized they were pilots.

"You speak English?" one asked.

"Yes, me speak little English."

"You Polski?"

"Yes, me Polski. Me work here. Me very happy. You are my friends."

One of them answered, "Yes. We're your friends, but don't tell anyone that we're here."

"No, no. Me don't tell. You my friends." Then, I asked, "You American pilots?"

One looked at the other and answered, "Yes."

"Are you hungry?" I asked.

"Yes. Can you help us?"

"Night, I bring you eat. Me go to work now. Must work fast."

"OK, Polski. We'd like to help you, too."

Then, they said to call them both Joe. They asked me my name.

"My name is Stanislaus."

"OK, Stanislaus."

They grabbed the bushel basket and loaded the wagon while I kept a lookout on the road. When they were done, I closed the door and left it unlocked. I might have lost some time but not enough to make Sossa suspicious. I didn't understand some of the words the Americans said, but I caught on to what they meant pretty well. Just before I left, they said loudly, "OK, the boy is all right." Then, they said, "Goodbye, Polski. We'll see you tonight." Their faces looked scared, though, worse than I was when they had the gun to my head.

I was glad that they believed me, and I urged the cows down the hill on the gravel road. As the wagon wheels creaked over the rocks, I thought, "This isn't a dream. It's real." It was the first time I'd seen American pilots. I had the courage to take care of these pilots. "I'll share my food or get some for them."

I'd share my food and help them even if the Germans found out. I didn't care about that anymore. After all, the pilots risked their lives to bring me freedom. "Dear God, don't let anyone find them here," I prayed. Even though the war was coming to an end, this was risky business for them and for me.

I was sure that, after the war, these airmen would help me kill all these Nazis.

I thought to myself over and over how good it was to know a few words of English, thanks to the lessons Maurice pressed into my head in the hospital. Those few words saved my life. How would they have been able to identify me as a friend otherwise? How good it was that I knew the Americans called the Germans "Krauts."

Hidden in the root cellar, I knew the pilots wouldn't bother anybody. The pilots were well-armed so I figured they'd be safe if someone from the Volkssturm should find them.

Right after work, I went to see Mike, the Russian, and asked him for bread and ham because he was always hiding food. Like me, he was never fed enough by the Germans. I told Mike that the Sossas had given me a very poor supper, and I was still hungry. I lied because I wouldn't dare to tell anybody about the pilots. Mike gave me the food, including some smoked meat, and I wrapped it into a bundle to take to the pilots. By this time, I was hiding packages of food from Sossa's cooler in the hay in the barn. I was glad to get the extra meat from Mike, but all I really needed from him was the bread because that was hard for me to sneak from Sossa's house. I put the bundle in the hay when I got home.

Then, I went upstairs to my room and waited for the hour when I'd visit the pilots. I was shaking with anxiety when I heard the tower clock chime the hour. I girded up my courage. I had told them I would come, and so I had to go. When I thought the time was right, I quietly left my room, went to the hay barn, and put the bundle under my arm. I cut across the fields, making a beeline for the root cellar.

As I approached from one side of the cave, I saw that the straw that blocked the air hole in winter had been disturbed. That must have been how the pilots got into the cellar. I checked the other air hole, and it also was messed up and a bit wet. I pulled out the straw and looked into the dark entrance. I kneeled and bent my head close to the hole, calling, "Joe, this is Polski."

Quietly, they answered, "Yes, Polski."

"Me have bread and ham," I said, and I handed the bundle through the hole to one of the airmen.

"OK, Polski," he said as he took it.

The only thing I wanted to do was to give them the package. I wasn't interested in talking because I probably wouldn't understand them, and besides, it would be hard to hear them talking from inside the root cellar. I just waited a moment to see if they wanted anything else. "You have water?" I asked.

"Yes."

Then, one of them crawled out with a pistol in his hand. He looked all around and said, "We have water. Thank you very much, Polski." He put his hand on my shoulder.

"Must go," I said, and I left.

I heard him say, "OK."

As I walked back to Sossa's, I felt lucky and pleased to have helped them. At last, I had done something to help the war effort. The second meeting was also at night and went even more smoothly because I had relaxed a bit. The first time I was there, I was shaking, hot, and scared. I could see death right in front of me. I found out that at night, the pilots would walk out to get water. There were plenty of water pumps for the gardens in the area.

At this time, the soil wasn't frozen. It looked like spring was on its way, and the farmers were beginning to work their fields. In the morning when I got up, I saw German trucks and soldiers all over the forest. They were hiding vehicles and tanks. There were tanks hiding even near Joe and Rita's house. This made my plans for bringing food to the pilots riskier. When I saw all this, I became very scared that the Germans might check over the root cellar. I prayed they wouldn't. The pilots observed all this military activity from the little hill in the field.

One day at lunch, Sossa mentioned that he had been in the root cellar. I must have gone completely pale with the news. My fork fell from my hand onto the plate. "Everything looked all right up there," he said. He didn't run into the pilots the way I had. If he had, he would have said goodbye to this world.

Despite the German soldiers, I brought a package of food to the pilots every fourth day. We didn't have any conversations, I just called Joe and passed the package through the hole.

The pilots told me they liked the meals. The food may not have been warm, but it was filling.

One night, things got complicated. After I'd left for the root cellar, Sossa decided to go to bed early. So he closed the gate and locked the door. When I got back and found the gate shut, it was easy for me to climb over, but getting into the house was another story. Sossa never gave me a key. I was lucky that there was an unlocked window in the washroom. The steel bars in the windows were just wide enough for me to slip through. I was lucky nobody saw me because anyone who had certainly would have wanted to know where I'd been. From then on, whenever I brought food to the pilots, I went to the washroom and made sure it was unlocked.

Finally, the German soldiers left Schrcenau with their tanks and trucks. I figured that more would come, but at least for a few days, we'd be rid of them. They pulled out on a Saturday, and that night, as usual, the villagers took bread and cake dough on plates to the bakery to be baked. When I saw Guedraut preparing the Sossa family's dough, I decided to steal one of the finished cakes from the bakery and share it with the pilots. These cakes were called Pfannekuchen, and looked like a cake pizza about twelve inches in diameter.

When it got dark, I went to the river, walked along the bank about a quarter-mile, and made a right turn through an opening that led straight to the back door of the bakery. The door wasn't closed, and the cakes were on the shelves. I took a large plate that held a cake and a loaf of bread. I don't know whose it was because it wasn't tagged. I was sure that the authorities wouldn't question everyone just for a missing cake. After all, everybody makes mistakes, and it would just look as though the baker misplaced the plate.

The goods were still warm as I hurried toward the river. Near the river bank, when I was sure I was far enough from the bakery not to be noticed, I cut the goods into four pieces, wrapped them in paper, and tied them with string. I took the big round plate the goodies came on and hurled it into the river. "Let your powerful currents take this plate far from here, river, and let the pilots and me have some of this cake."

I took the package to them, and we ate it together.

"It's good, Polski. Thank you very much."

"You're welcome," I said.

That was the last time I saw the pilots, just a few days before the Americans came.

Thirteen

LITTLE GIRL TOYS

THE Germans were on the retreat, pulling their forces deeper into Germany. We could hear the cannons as the Germans and Allies clashed in the distance. A couple of days later, German soldiers took over the forest and Schrcenau. They stayed for a few days, and then backed out of the village and over the Main river bridge in a great hurry, as if someone were chasing them. Their tanks and trucks left deep ruts and holes in the road. The soldiers left lice all over the benches and chairs in Sossa's tavern. Guedraut had to sweep everything with a broom and then disinfect the whole area.

The German soldiers weren't in foreign countries where they could beat women into washing their clothes for nothing anymore. Those good times for the German soldiers were over. They couldn't beat their own women into washing clothes for them. So their clothes were infested.

A week later, another group of soldiers pulled into Schrcenau. They were all over the village and the forest. The artillery was becoming louder and louder as the Allied front moved toward us. American fighter planes dotted the sky like birds. Artillery shells were falling on some nearby villages. Some hit homes.

"We are finished," I heard a German soldier say. "We don't have any more power."

The German civilians were saying that they weren't going to work now. "Who do we work for?" they asked.

The Gestapo said, "We haven't lost the war yet. We'll push these devils back where they belong!"

More SS came the next day. They were on foot, carrying ammunition, bazookas, and machine guns on their backs. They were tired and stopped for rest. They forced their way into homes, and the civilians had to feed them. They walked back and forth through the village and put down their ammunition anywhere they could. Many of them went for beer in the tavern. Others just rested on the street.

By day's end, they had dragged in a mess wagon and parked it by Sossa's tavern. Pistols were hanging everywhere, even in the back yard of the tavern. They laid ammunition on window sills and fences. When I looked at those pistols, I gulped hard. "I only want one pistol, that's all," I told myself. "Should I take one? I may need it in the future." I came to a decision. "No, don't take it. They might blame Sossa, and that would mean trouble for me. I'd better wait. Maybe I'll have a better chance later. It looks to me like they're going to make their stand against the Allies right here in Schrcenau."

Their officers were staying at Nina's, and she had to feed them. Nina heard one of the German officers say they planned to fight right in Schrcenau. Nina protested. "You can't fight here! You'll destroy the villages! You can't stop the Americans anymore."

One of the high-ranking officers said, "You're not going to stop me." He shoved her and she fell. Angrily, he pulled out his pistol and aimed to shoot her, but another officer stepped in and knocked the gun aside. The bullet crashed into a wall. The angry officer left Nina's, and the others followed him into the street. After about a half an hour, Nina got up off the floor. Still in shock, she stayed in the rest of the day. Her boys were telling this story to the villagers only minutes after she got up.

About an hour after the incident, everyone got the word that the troops were pulling out. Trucks, cannons, vehicles, men, and even the mess wagon began moving across the Main river bridge. This time, poor Guedraut had to sweep the lice from the SS. Lice were all over the floor. She called me in to show me how the lice had taken over like never before. She swept benches, tables and chairs, and had to fumigate the tavern.

Scattered units of German soldiers and their trucks and jeeps took over the village again. They slept in barns and drank in the tavern. One night, a soldier slept in Sossa's barn. When he heard the artillery closing in the next morning, he got up without his helmet on and walked out. I saw him leave so fast he didn't even button his coat. When I went to feed the cows, I saw that he'd left his rifle and bayonet in the hay. I spread hay over it and wondered whether the soldier would come back for it. All day, I walked back and forth to see if the rifle was still there. I figured I might need the rifle before this mess was over. When the soldier didn't come back by nightfall, I claimed the rifle as mine.

I hurried out to the hay barn and found a good spot to hide it. One day, I took the rifle up into the hayloft, where there was a skylight. I opened the rifle and found bullets in the chamber. I removed them. I looked down from the loft, and there was no one around. I pointed the rifle at a corner of the barn. Then, I pulled the trigger to make sure there were no bullets hiding in the chamber. Nothing came out. I didn't know much about the gun, so I closed the chamber, took off the bayonet, and hid them in the hay.

There wasn't much to do the next day. Almost all the villagers and we foreigners were not working. It was like a strike. So I went up to the hayloft again. I tried to get acquainted with the rifle.

I handled it very delicately, opened the chamber, pointed at the corner once again, and pulled the trigger to make sure that it wasn't loaded. I took the gun apart and cleaned the parts. I used some light oil to shine the barrel. I put it back together and pulled the trigger to see if it still worked. Everything was fine. I wrapped it all up in a little blanket this time and hid it back in the hay. Now, I could protect myself.

I didn't have many bullets for this rifle, so I had to think of a way to get more. By the gate where the soldiers were going back and forth to the tavern, the troops had laid boxes of ammunition on a window sill so they wouldn't have to carry them wherever they went. They'd rest, go into the tavern, and then come out to rest again. I had to get those bullets, but it was scary. The soldiers were all over. If one of them saw me taking the ammo, they'd ask dangerous questions.

I had an idea when I saw Hilda, Guedraut's five-year-old niece. I called to her, and she came over to me. I held her by the hand and said, "Do you see those boxes on the window sill? They're wonderful toys. Would you go over there and get me two boxes of those toys? That way you can have some, too. I'll show you how to play with them."

Hilda was a very helpful little girl, and she listened carefully. "Are those toys on the window sill?"

"Yes," I said, "bring me two boxes of them."

"Yes, Stanislaus. I'll go get them."

I watched every move she made. If she got caught, they'd probably figure she was just a little girl who didn't know what she was playing with. She reached for one box at a time and came back to me with two of them. I took the boxes and said, "Go back where you were playing. Later, I'll show you how to play with these." Everything turned out OK. She went back to play in the back yard, and I hid the boxes in the hayloft near the rifle. I took out some of the bullets to see if they were the right ones. I tried them in the chamber, and they fit. Then I hid everything I'd taken out in the hay.

When I came down the ladder from the hayloft, I saw that soldiers had left many boxes of bullets where the wagon was standing. I quietly collected about ten more boxes. I figured that would be enough for a long time.

The German units left the villages and crossed the bridge over the Main. Later, five German trucks came to Schrcenau to drop off uniforms, all new, at the tavern. Everything was brought upstairs to the dance hall, where Sossa kept his big bottles of schnapps. They were in a big hurry, and when they were done, they too headed across the Main.

Things were changing quickly. Every hour, it seemed, there was a new development. The villagers didn't know what to do with themselves. Some packed their belongings in boxes, and others were already heading to the forest. Others waited in their back yards to see what would happen here. After all, who knew where it would be safe? We foreigners didn't even think about what would happen to us. We weren't worried. What will be, will be. All the foreign workers in Schrcenau, especially the Polish and French POWs, stayed together in big groups. Nobody did any work except to feed the animals. So far, all the German soldiers and vehicles had gone over the bridge to the other side of the Main.

It was a scary time, and nobody knew what would happen next.

Fourteen

———THOMAS AND BIG STANISLAUS———

AFTER Kessler beat me up over the cigarettes, I rarely talked to Thomas, who instigated the whole incident. I didn't want to be his friend, but I did say hello sometimes. Thomas started talking to me, though. I think he still felt guilty, but I think he also smelled schnapps. He knew Sossa made the stuff, and he also knew that I didn't have a very good suit for social events like dances. I had outgrown the suit I had. The pants I was wearing were short, and the sleeves of the coat were too short and tight. The back of the coat was ripping apart, and I couldn't even button it anymore. Because I wasn't earning any money, I couldn't buy myself a new one. Sossa could have given me a suit that one of his sons had outgrown, but he didn't care how I looked.

So, sometime before life in the villages was completely disrupted by the Allied advance, Thomas proposed a deal. He'd give me a suit he'd outgrown for two liters of schnapps. "Give me the schnapps, and I'll give you the suit." I didn't trust Thomas, but I needed the suit so badly that I agreed to get him the schnapps.

It wasn't hard for me to get the schnapps from Sossa's dance hall, even though it was locked. There was an opening over the counter that they used for passing beer into the dance hall. It was blocked with glasses and jars, and the window was closed from the side I slept on. The window was always open before the war. The whole counter where the barrels of beer sat was filled with jars and bottles now. So was the bar.

Late one night, when everybody was sleeping, I started to move the jars. Although it was dark, the street light shining through the window made it bright enough to work. I took the jars down one by one and put them aside on the floor. It was a very delicate job. It took me two hours because I had to make sure the glass jars didn't hit one another. If one jar fell or hit another, it would wake up everyone.

I easily slipped through the window into the dance hall. I uncorked one of Sossa's schnapps bottles. I pulled out a glass pitcher that easily could have held three liters. I tipped over the big bottle and filled up the pitcher with schnapps. I put the cork back on the bottle and very gently slid the pitcher through the window. I held it carefully so it wouldn't spill or make a noise. I was very lucky. Nothing went wrong. I put the pitcher under my bed, where I had hidden three one-liter bottles several days earlier. Then, I started to put all those jars back where they belonged. When I was finished with that, I used a funnel to pour the schnapps from the pitcher into the liter bottles. I hid those in the attic, putting them between other bottles that were up there so they'd be hard to spot. I wiped the pitcher and put it back where it belonged under the buffet. After all that work, I went to bed. As I drifted off, I thought to myself, "At least I got something for all my hard work and the beating I took from Alexander." I felt my blood was paid for with the three liters of schnapps.

Late on a Saturday night, I took two liters of schnapps — I kept the other liter for myself — to Thomas's room at Nina's farm. He took the schnapps from me and tasted it. "That's good," he said.

"Now give me the suit," I said.

"You know, Stanislaus, I have to clean that suit before I give it to you." I knew right away he was lying.

After lunch one day, I saw Thomas wearing the pants from the suit as he went out to do some work in the field. I stopped him on the gravel road by Sossa's potato field. "Thomas, are you wearing the pants that you were supposed to give me?"

"Yes," he said.

"You are a liar!" I said. "Your words are evil! How could you cheat a small boy like me? Why don't you be sensible and make the trade you promised?" I spit on his feet and said, "Think about it! Come to your senses and give me the suit! It wouldn't be hard to just give me the suit! Try it, Thomas!"

"Shut your mouth, you punk!" Thomas said angrily. "I'm going to tell Sossa that you stole the schnapps!"

"Sure! I'm waiting for that! What could I expect? Go ahead and tell him whatever you want! Go to him right now if you want! But remember this, we will meet again!"

Thomas spoke more loudly, "You punk!" He tried to grab me by the shirt, but I backed away from his grasp.

That evening after work, I went to see Big Stanislaus. He had chewed Thomas out before because Thomas laughed when I was smacked around by the Nazis. Maybe Big Stanislaus wasn't my friend, but he'd shown me some sympathy before, and maybe he could help me in this situation. I told him about how Thomas had reneged on the deal for the suit. So Big Stanislaus put on his shirt and said, "What a rotten guy! Taking the schnapps from you and then wearing the suit pants to work! Let's go see Thomas!"

When we entered Thomas's room, Big Stanislaus grabbed Thomas by his collar. "Very nice trick you pulled on this little guy! Then calling him names and still not giving him the suit! If you go to Sossa and tell him about the schnapps, I'm going to strangle you!"

Big Stanislaus loosened his grip and said, "Where's the suit? Where's the schnapps? Put everything on the table so I can see it!"

Thomas hung his head, but he brought out the schnapps and put the suit coat on the table. He was still wearing the pants.

"What else do you want from me?" Thomas said.

"What do I want from you? I'd like to taste that schnapps. Is it any good?" He uncorked the bottled and took a swig. "Oh! Oh! Oh! Good schnapps!"

Thomas piped up, "I was going to give him the suit, but I wanted to clean it first because there are some spots on it!"

Big Stanislaus laughed. "You can tell that to some-body else, not me. I don't buy that! You made a deal with the boy for two liters of schnapps. Right, Thomas?"

"Yes."

"Then put that suit on the table right this minute. I want to see you give it to him with my own eyes!"

Thanks to Big Stanislaus, I got the suit that night.

I decided to go to Big Stanislaus because I didn't want to keep my resentment of Thomas inside, where it would eat me up. It felt good to express myself and to get results.

Before I left, Thomas said, "I'm very sorry."

He never spoke to me again, which was OK with me. Thomas learned something that evening, though. He started to understand things. It took him quite awhile to respect his brothers, the Polish men. Eventually, when he talked with them, he spoke with respect.

Guedraut cleaned and pressed the suit for me about a week later. Finally, I had something good to wear when I went out socially.

The whole time I was in Germany, I had been very good at keeping secrets. I was a very secretive young man, but soon after the German soldiers started retreating through Schrcenau, I let it slip to Big Stanislaus that I had a rifle and bullets. He paid some attention to me then and began talking to me about it.

He said, "I'd like to have a rifle like that myself. I'll probably need one sometime soon."

I told him not to get any ideas about taking the rifle from me. "The rifle is going to stay in my hands. I'll need it for my safety in the future."

This was sometime in March 1945, when everyone was waiting for the Americans to come in. One day, the villagers started rushing back and forth excitedly. Shortly after, everything got quiet. The word had come through that the Volkssturm had disbanded. The German soldiers in town immediately took off and crossed the Main bridge. The American front was closing in from the west. I could hear their machine guns and cannons. Then, they stopped, still on this side of the Main.

The next day was Saturday, and things were quiet. On Sunday afternoon, though, activity picked up again. Everybody was rushing this way and that. There was a lot of traffic.

The mayor had a message for the villagers. Two ladies rang a bell and read the mayor's message into a microphone. I thought, "This is the last time that guy will give any orders to the people."

We didn't know if the orders came from higher up or if the mayor and Kessler came up with the idea by themselves. His orders were that all the foreign workers had to report in front of Sossa's tavern and bring picks and shovels with them.

The mayor stood outside Sossa's in a Nazi uniform. Kessler was there too. The main road from Dettelbach to Schwarca was paved. The mayor and Kessler ordered us to dig post holes deep on both sides of the road. The German civilians were told to go into the forest and cut trees and bring them to where we were digging. Another post hole was dug in the center of the road. The villagers had to cut the trees to a certain length and then set them in the holes. They filled the holes in with stones and dirt. The thick timber the German men set in the holes stood at least ten feet high. Smaller logs were nailed to these big posts. When they were done with the barrier, they spread out a whole roll of barbed wire atop it. Kessler and the mayor thought the barricade would foul up the American advance. When it was finished, the mayor said, "That should be strong enough to hold the American dogs."

We foreigners weren't happy with this, but we didn't have any choice. The mayor and Kessler still had power. When the barricade was completed, the pair left for the priest's house. From what I heard, a high-ranking German officer, who had gone AWOL, was there. He came home on a furlough and never returned to his unit. The mayor and Kessler had had their eyes on him for a while and finally arrested him. Now they were going to bring him to the Kitzingen jail.

While Kessler and the mayor went about that business, the villagers broke the barricade apart and took the logs home for firewood. They dismantled the barbed wire and rolled it back up. The barricade was gone. The mayor and Kessler couldn't retaliate because there were too many against them. I couldn't believe what I saw, what a bunch of villagers could do. We foreigners stood on the street and talked about how strange it was to see the German villagers stick up for themselves.

The mayor was angry and came up with another plan to hold off the Americans. That evening, some French POWs taking a walk saw him plant an explosive charge on the first post on the west side of the bridge. When he realized that people had seen him, he let the word out to the villagers that the charge was set to blow at 6 a.m.

Almost everybody had trouble sleeping because of this news. I got up early the next day. It was a bit cloudy and raining a little. I opened the small iron gate and stood there looking around for a while.

When I looked down the road, I spotted a jeep coming from the west. It was an American vehicle on its way to the bridge. The Americans looked funny to me because their helmets and uniforms were different from the German styles I was used to. There was a big white star on the side of the vehicle. Two American soldiers sat in the front, and a third was standing in the back holding his hand on the trigger of a machine gun. I wasn't scared. I just stood there resting and said nothing. The driver stopped about two yards away from me and asked in English, "Where are the German soldiers?"

"All German soldiers are kaput," I answered. I pointed toward the bridge. The driver pointed in the same direction, drove past me toward the bridge, and turned around in a wide spot in the road. He came back past me. I figured they were only scouting the situation, and I didn't say anything more. The jeep headed back toward Dettelbach. I went to the barn to feed the cows.

A little more than a half-hour later, the jeep came back, followed by a number of trucks, soldiers, other jeeps, gasoline trucks, and other military vehicles. They were coming down the hill toward the bridge.

The first jeep drove by me. A captain, lieutenant, and machine gunner were aboard. I raised my hands and said, "Me Polski!"

The captain said, "Put your hands down! Where are the Germans?"

"Over the bridge! No go! No go! Bridge explode! Captain, go back west! Bridge explode! What time is it?"

He said, "Seven minutes to six."

"Bridge explode!" I held up seven fingers to try to explain the bridge would explode in just seven minutes. We stopped in front of the priest's house. We were still talking, and I wasn't sure if they'd understood me. As long as they stood there, though, they were safe. The blast wouldn't reach that far. As they talked, the captain would glance at the tower clock. I looked back at the line of vehicles and soldiers. They were all looking at me. The men in the lead jeep gave me another look, too. Just then, the bomb went off.

The Americans smiled and cheered! "Thanks, Polski! Thanks again!"

They backed out and turned around, starting back to Dettelbach. They all waved to me and said, "Goodbye, Polski! OK! OK!" Then, they were on their way. I was happy and proud of myself. It was the happiest day of my life so far. I finally got to see the American soldiers.

I was thinking so hard as I walked back from the priest's house that I passed the gate. I had followed the Americans a whole block before I realized it. Maybe it was a good thing because then I realized how close I was to the root cellar. I ran there to let the American pilots know what was happening. I looked into the open hole and called, "Joe! Joe!" The pilots weren't there.

As I went back to Sossa's, I wondered whether the pilots had headed out to the American front or whether the Germans had captured them. I knew they wouldn't be able to say goodbye. Still, I felt anxious and heart-sick wondering about where they'd gone. Whatever happened, I hoped they were with the American soldiers. "God bless them and help them," I thought. I was glad I'd had the chance to help them.

Fifteen

DARK NIGHT OF THE KILLER

FINALLY, the balance of the scale was tipping away from the Germans. We had waited long and patiently for this day. The scale was pretty well balanced now, and soon it would tip in favor of the Americans.

This was early spring, and everything was quiet. All was silence; even the birds weren't singing. Nothing was certain yet, but it sure looked like the Americans were winning. A jeep carrying American officers came to check out the damage to the bridge, the only path across the Main. All day, villagers came out to see the damaged bridge, too.

That evening, when it wasn't quite dark, I lay in bed, not yet asleep. All of a sudden, I heard Sossa's wife. Then, in a minute, someone was running upstairs to my room like he wanted to kill me. I was scared to death. From under the bed, I pulled out an emergency rope I had tied underneath there. I opened the window and threw it out. The coil unraveled right to the ground. I was ready to climb out the window, when there was a heavy knocking on my door. I didn't answer.

"Stanislaus! It's me, Big Stanislaus! Open the door!" I breathed a little easier when I recognized his voice. Then, I opened the door. Big Stanislaus entered like he was crazy, running and out of breath. He said, "Get dressed quickly! Where do you have that gun? We're going to the priest's house!"

I said, "To the priest's house? What for?"

"Don't ask any questions! Just get moving!"

"I don't want to go anywhere!" I said.

Big Stanislaus picked me up by the front of my clothes. "You punk! You want me to punch you? You want to wait till the Germans come up here and kill you?"

I had no choice. I put my shoes on, pulled the rope back up, threw it under the bed, and closed the window.

"Come on! Come on!" Big Stanislaus said.

We walked down the stairs from my room and went to the barn. I climbed to the loft and got the rifle and ammo. After we came out of the barn, Big Stanislaus grabbed the rifle out of my hands and five boxes of bullets. He strapped the rifle over his shoulder and ran through the back yard and gate like someone was chasing him. As we moved to the iron gate, Sossa, his wife, and Guedraut were looking at us. They said nothing. I was wondering what they were thinking about me, especially about me having a rifle.

We went to the second floor of the priest's house. I was surprised to see a lot of people there. I knew most of them. Rifles and shotguns lay on the table. Big Stanislaus put my rifle down on the table, too. The priest stood behind the table, next to a high-ranking German officer, the one Kessler and the mayor had taken to Kitzingen the day before.

Also in the room, I saw some French POWs, Thomas, and other Polish men from the village. Everybody was shaken, and I still didn't know what was going on or why the German officer was present. The priest and the officer were showing everybody how to operate the weapons spread out on the table. The guns were all pointing toward the priest and the officer. Big Stanislaus was probably the only person, other than those two, who knew what was going on.

The officer gave a speech to let everyone know what was up. "Please, don't be afraid of me! I won't hurt you men! I came here because I don't know where else to go! I'm in as much danger as you are! I came here on furlough to see my girlfriend, and I didn't go back like I was supposed to. I could see that the war was going to end. Especially when I got to Dettelbach and saw that the bombardment was as bad as my girlfriend said in her letters.

"I got caught in an air raid there. I was covered in rubble and took some shrapnel in my ribs. People dug me out and took me to the hospital. They patched me up and said I was OK, and I came on to Schrcenau to see my girlfriend. As you know, I was arrested as a deserter. I was supposed to be shot in Kitzingen this morning.

"By some miracle, I had a chance to escape through the rubble of the buildings and factories this morning.

The guards wounded me in my hands as I escaped. It was hard to walk, I felt weak and blood was dripping from my wounds, but I really wanted to get to Schrcenau. I had just crossed the bridge when it blew up, almost under my feet. What bad luck!

"The priest and I will show you how to work these weapons, how to load the ammunition, and you'll get a little practice. There are enough guns for everybody. When we're done, we're going to hunt down the mayor and Kessler. I know that you feel about them the same way I do. Don't kill them if you can avoid it, but shoot them in the stomach if you have to shoot. I hope we find them, but be careful because they have good weapons."

The officer was in bad shape, and I didn't think he was going to come with us, but he said he would. The priest did the best he could, sharing his guns. He showed us how to work them. He knew very well that these two Nazis, the mayor and Kessler, had to be stopped or killed, no matter what.

My eyes landed on my rifle. I wanted to make sure that no one else took it because I liked it and it was mine. I got close to the table and placed my hand on the rifle. "I'm going to take this one because I already know how to use it."

Big Stanislaus heard what I said and told me, "Be patient. Don't be nervous." As he said it, I pulled the chamber open. I didn't see any bullets in there, and I pulled the trigger. The rifle was still on the table, pointed in the officer's direction. It fired. Big Stanislaus must have put a bullet in. When he took the gun, it was empty. I knew that because I had just cleaned it and put it away empty.

173

The bullet went right through the officer's heart. He managed to ask, "What are you doing?" and then slumped over the table. There was a sudden movement among the men. "Did someone shoot the officer?" someone asked.

"Yes. I did it," I said. "But it was an accident. I didn't know there was a bullet in the chamber."

The officer's head was on the table. His girlfriend was bending over, right by his head, and crying mournfully. I can still hear his last words, "What are you doing?"

Suddenly, everyone was running into the hall and down the stairs. "Who knows what kind of trouble we're in now!" someone said. "We've got to get away from this village!"

All the weapons were forgotten, except mine. Thomas took it and some bullets. Everyone was scared as they ran. They jumped over fences and ran through bushes in their haste to get away. Some of the German villagers came out of their houses, screaming. "We heard a shot! Was it the priest?"

The night was very dark and cold, with a light drizzle to boot. I wondered what I was going to do. I decided I had to run, too. "I'm not going to stay here."

Big Stanislaus ran and jumped a big fence. I went after him. He spotted me and said, "Don't follow me! I don't want to see you, you killer! Go the other way somewhere! I wouldn't wish meeting you again on anybody!" My shoes were all muddy, the rain was still falling, and I was cold. Big Stanislaus kept talking, "The field is very big and wide! Choose your own path! We can't be together! We can't be in a pack! Do you understand that?"

174

"Don't be afraid," I said. "I won't get you killed! I don't need your help! I'll be all right!"

"Go toward the American front," he yelled. "That's the only choice you have!"

He went his way, and I went mine.

I went to the root cellar. Maybe the American pilots had come back since I looked in on them in the daytime. "They'll help me for sure," I thought.

I came to the hole in the cellar and called, "Joe." No answer. Then, I crawled into the cellar, looked around, and again called out, "Joe." Nobody was there, I was sure. I didn't light the candle, though. I was scared that maybe some German retreating from the front was around. I called out once more. "Joe. Joe, help me!" But it was to no avail.

I cried because they were gone. How could I blame them, though? They had to take care of themselves.

Scared, I crawled out the window and stuffed the straw back into it. I told myself, "I'm alone now, and I'll have to pick my own road to walk tonight." The thoughts in my head were killing me. I was a killer now, but only by accident. I should have been more careful, but I didn't know Big Stanislaus had put bullets in the chamber. I hadn't planned to kill anyone, especially not the officer. Still, nobody believed me. It happened. It really happened. The officer was dead and would never get up, but his spirit was dragging me all over the field. I was completely lost in the same field I had been walking for two years. Even though I knew it like the back of my hand, at this point in the dark night, I was completely lost. I kept walking around in circles.

My mind kept repeating the words: "Go toward the front." I tried to travel that way, but for some reason, I kept ending up back in the same spot. I feared that some Germans who would try to hold the American front would capture me. I didn't know whether the last German soldier had pulled out from the west, or even whether they were advancing again. Life gets complicated on the front, my father once told me. I could run into a single soldier or a whole battalion.

Still, I decided once more that I must head west, but I couldn't even tell which way west was. I couldn't tell in the darkness. I couldn't stop traveling in a circle. It was like there was no way out.

I sat a on a creek bank and talked to myself. "Where am I? Where did this creek come from?" I took out my pocket knife. It was clean and shiny. A little voice in my head said, "Kill yourself!" I screamed, "No! I can't! I can't do that. I've got to follow the plan and head west!" Then, to protect myself, I threw the knife into the dirt where I wouldn't be able to find it in the dark. I screamed. I didn't care if anyone heard me. Again, I screamed. "Get away from me, you devil! I don't want you around! I didn't kill that officer! It was an accident!" I made the sign of the cross.

I stretched myself in the black mud like a cross, and I fixed my eyes on the dark heavens. I said loud and clear, "Oh, God! Give me the strength to get through this jam so I can go where I'm supposed to go! I can't go to church, but I believe in you in my mind. I know you're with me here! Forgive me for what I've done." Still lying there, I dug into the dirt with both hands. Then, I sat up, raising the two handfuls, and said, "You beautiful soil! You've taken millions of people and covered them with dirt. Take me, oh beautiful soil! Cover me! I don't want to live anymore!"

The rain stopped, but it was still storming in the area. Lightning kept flashing. I looked in the direction of the lightning and saw what appeared to be a group of German soldiers scattered about, guards walking back and forth. "Oh, my God! They probably heard me when I screamed!" I immediately hit the dirt again and lay still, my eyes trained in their direction.

I inched my way across the mud a few yards, trying to get farther away, but the Germans were walking in the same direction. "The guards see me," I thought. I lay on the ground an hour, waiting for something to happen. I started to shake from the cold. My teeth chattered. "I can't stay like this any longer," I thought. "I'm going to be sick for sure. I can't run, they might shoot me. I have to surrender."

I got up on my feet and put my hands in the air. I walked toward the German soldiers. I screamed with all my might, "Don't shoot! Don't shoot! I surrender! I have my hands up and don't have any weapons. I didn't plan to kill that officer. Forgive me that mistake. Don't shoot! Give me the chance to see my parents again!"

I had walked forward about ten yards. There was no shooting. I didn't see any guns. What I had seen wasn't a soldier. It was a wooden cross. I came from behind the cross and saw a very wide road. Right away I knew where I was. "No," I said. There had never been a cross in this spot before. I knew the road very well, a gravel road that headed west. Then, I had to believe my eyes. "Yes. It's a cross by the road, but what kind of cross?" I couldn't see who or what was on the cross. I just looked at the wood. I didn't try to touch it. I just stood there two meters from it. From that moment, I felt different. I felt like I wasn't lost anymore. I wasn't scared of this cross I had never seen before because I felt that God was there, leading me to the road. I felt he had forgiven my sins. There'd be no more of my screaming. I made the sign of the cross and headed west.

I was free. The weight was off my shoulders. I didn't feel any more guilt in my mind or my heart. Maybe it was a good thing that the officer died that way. I didn't want to shoot him, but I kept him from going any further with his plans to get the mayor and Kessler. Maybe during the war, he'd killed many people and he thought that carrying out his plan would save him from jail after the war. Even if he wanted to do something to help the foreigners and the Americans, he could have cost us all our lives by going ahead with his plan. We heard the Germans were shooting all foreigners before they left the front. The officer just came to bad luck all around.

The wide gravel road ended. I was no longer lost. I went through a field in a straight line toward the American front. I walked through fields almost the whole night. Close to daylight, I felt very tired. I heard the artillery, louder and louder. I could hear many machine guns firing, but it was difficult to tell how far from the American front I was. Finally, I spotted a barn on a small farm. As I approached the property's fence, the farmer's dog began barking. The farmer came outside to check on what was going on. Fortunately, I saw him coming. I walked back a little bit and stooped down. The farmer walked close by my hiding place, but he didn't spot anything. The dog was still barking, but the farmer went back inside. I think he went back to bed because it was still a little early to get up.

I didn't wait too long. I had to move before daylight. I crawled into the barn from the side away from the dog and the house. I buried myself in the straw and got ready to sleep. The dog stopped barking. I could still here artillery shells falling. I wasn't very warm when I nestled in there, but the straw felt good, and I began to warm up a little. I fell asleep right away. I don't know how long I slept. I didn't have a watch.

I slept until I heard someone opening the barn door. The door squeaked, and I heard the farmer coming. I buried myself deeper in the straw. He came over and jabbed his fork into the straw and almost got me on the leg. I moved it out of the way quickly. I saw him leave the barn with a bundle of straw over his shoulder. He was headed to the cow barn. I got out of the straw very quickly. I shook the straw off my clothes as well as I could. Then I sneaked out to the gravel road.

I looked in both directions and couldn't figure out which way was west. It was cloudy but warmer than the day before. I waited for the sun to come out from behind the clouds and figured I'd walk away from the morning sun to head west. The sun came out ever so slowly. I begged the sun to come out. "Please, come out and make me warm. At least for an hour, take the chill off the morning."

I had walked quite awhile, when I saw a middle-age woman coming toward me. A Polish proverb says that when you see a woman so early in the morning, the day will go to hell. I thought about that but then said, "Luck or no luck. What will be, will be." I decided to ask her where I was and whether she'd seen any American soldiers.

As politely and gently as I could, I said, "Good morning."

"Good morning, young man," she answered.

We talked, and she gave me very good news. The Americans were in Dettelbach, just four kilometers from this spot. Then, she pointed me in the right direction. The woman never asked me any questions, even though I was dirty and had straw all over my hair and clothes. I thanked her and began walking toward Dettelbach.

I figured I had walked about eighteen kilometers. I cut through the plowed fields. I kept walking, trying to keep warm. As I got closer to Dettelbach, I beat the mud off my shoes and shook the straw off my jacket. I wiped my face and hands with my handkerchief. I cleaned myself up the best I could because I wanted to look good when I saw a truck with a big white star.

I was coming into the northwest side of town. I was probably the first man to see the Americans come. It was the first time I'd seen an American tank. A whole unit followed the tank. "I made it," I told myself. "I finally made it."

Some Americans stopped. I said, "Hello, Americans. Hello." I asked, "Do you speak Polish?"

One of them said, "Yes, I speak Polish." Then, he asked me in Polish if I was hungry. I told him I was, and he passed me an opened can of ham, an orange, and some crackers.

I said, "Thank you." I left the Americans and walked down a gravel road to a barn. I sat down and started to eat. Boy! That tasted good. I hadn't eaten anything since the day before.

I walked into Dettelbach and met many Poles. They had come from other towns. A group of them asked me to come along with them as they went to celebrate the American victory. We ate and drank wine. It was a real celebration. I slept with them in a barn overnight.

Sixteen

STANISLAUS'S REVENGE

THE American tanks stood on German soil. I watched a tank make a few different turns in a field. It made a big hole, as if to say to the Germans, "We're here!" The time had come for a wave of fresh air, so we could breathe freely again.

Many thousands of civilians, many thousand American soldiers, and many thousand German troops had been killed in this war. Death is the price of war, but none of us saw any reason for the Germans to have tortured civilians — women, children, and old people. There was no reason for the experiments on people, for the way they made gloves and other products from human skin. There was no reason for the German soldiers and officers to rape women on the front, sometimes torturing and killing them.

These thoughts went through my head as I stood on the road and looked at the American soldiers, who were very far away from their free country. I was so happy, I almost jumped up on the tank to go away with them. I knew that I'd have to wait a long time before the world got back to normal and there'd be a road open back to Poland. The celebration of the day before continued. I ran into many Poles who had worked in nearby villages, as well as Poles who'd worked in Schrcenau. I ran into Big Stanislaus during the celebration, and he told me, "If I were you, I'd hide somewhere. The Americans might shoot you for killing that officer. They have a different law."

I thought, "What will be, will be."

Johann, an older man who'd worked in Schrcenau, was very understanding. He told me I should go with him to another village where he had a friend. Because the front wasn't advancing yet, he said the farther west we went, the safer we would be.

Johann also tried to comfort me over the officer's death. "His death probably happened for the best. We could have followed him, and we could have all been killed." He also didn't think much of what Big Stanislaus had told me. "This is still war time! Nothing's going to happen to you for killing a German officer during the war."

I agreed to go with him to the other village. We figured it was sixteen kilometers to get there, which was quite far to walk. We were wondering what we'd do when we saw a German on a bicycle. We suspected he was a deserter because he wore German army boots with civilian clothes. Johann turned to me and said, "We're going to knock that Kraut off his bike. You're a small boy. Do you remember what the Germans did when they came to Poland? How they robbed us of everything?"

"Yes, Johann," I said, "I remember."

"Now, it's our turn," Johann said.

We ran at the German and knocked him off his bicycle. He didn't try to fight back. He was scared. The German didn't say a word.

Johann didn't know how to ride a bicycle, so he asked if I knew.

"I've been riding since I was five years old," I told him.

Johann sat on the bar, and I got on the seat and pedaled like crazy until we reached the village. I was sweating from the exercise. Thank God, we made it. The day was clear, calm, and warm, and it was already the afternoon when we arrived. In one spot, many nationalities gathered — men and women, all holding glasses and drinking wine. They were drinking heavily. We got off the bike and joined the crowd. People greeted us warmly, and they offered us food and drink. We answered all their questions about what we'd been through. Johann even talked about the shooting of the German officer. They agreed with Johann that things could have turned out differently if I hadn't shot him. Everybody drank to freedom and to those who were still alive.

After a couple of days of celebration, we were a little shaky. Johann and I got on the bike and headed to Wurzburg, where we got some food and American orange juice. The Americans fed us and treated us very well. After eating, we rested on some park benches. Then we got on the bicycle and headed back to Schrcenau. It was many kilometers, but we made it that day. Everything in Schrcenau seemed to be in order, nice and quiet. The front was very far east of us, all the way to Regensburg by the river. Johann took the bicycle to the farm where he was working, and I went back to Sossa's.

It had been five days since the officer was killed, and it looked as though everybody was coming back to Schrcenau to work. I didn't have to work as hard as I did before, though. I just had to help. Sossa didn't push anybody, even when I slept a little longer — and I still got my meals.

The officer was buried the same day Joe was buried. My little friend had found a bazooka after the German soldiers left. When he started to take it apart, it exploded and cut him to pieces. Sossa told me about it the day after I returned to the farm. I couldn't be there when they buried him, in the same cemetery as the seven American airmen. I looked at the cemetery and prayed for the airmen, the officer, and Joe. I didn't go see Rita or her mother because I didn't want to upset them all over again. It was such a terrible accident. I thought about how Joe's father had been killed on the Russian front, and now Joe had joined him in heaven.

A couple of days after I returned, I spoke with the Catholic priest. The priest said he was always on my side, and he wanted to help me as much as he could to get those two killers, the mayor and Kessler. He knew how much they'd beaten me up and how much of my health they stole. I also heard about the mayor. After he dynamited the bridge, he walked over to the other side of the river. Near the turn in the river where I almost drowned, he shot himself. He was afraid of the

German civilians and the others because he had killed some prisoners and some foreigners. He couldn't live in those villages anymore. He took himself off my list.

I tried to hunt Kessler down. I thought he was hiding somewhere in the night hours, but I had no luck. I thought maybe someday I'd find him. I wished I still had my rifle. I wanted it just for Kessler. At this point, there was nothing for me to do but wait and see. I figured we'd meet again, and he stayed on my list.

I marked Nina off my list because she got her share when the German officer shoved her down and almost killed her. That was enough for her. Besides, she was the mother of two nice boys.

One day I spotted the leader of the Hitler Youth gang, a boy named Miller. He lived on the west side of the river, in a tower by the bridge. His father's job was to monitor the ships and freighters that went by. He was also a fisherman. They owned some boats, which they kept on the river. After the bridge was blown up, the big boy would ferry people across the river for money. One evening, after this boy finished his job, I was waiting for him where the boat was anchored.

"Give me a ride to the other side of the river," I told him.

"For you? Never. I already finished my job for tonight."

He turned his back, and I said, "It's very important for me to get across. I have to meet someone at Schwarca."

The big boy didn't want to do it, but he gave in. He got me to the other side of the river and didn't even ask me for a fare, but he wanted to get away from me.

"Come with me!" I said. "Come with me. Pull the boat up on the bank."

"I'm not going anywhere," he said.

I grabbed him by the front of his shirt and put my bayonet to his throat. "Now you're mine!" He was bigger and older than the last time I saw him, but I wasn't afraid. This guy didn't want to tangle with me, so he did what I told him. I held him by the sleeve of his coat and put the bayonet to his ribs. Then, we walked out onto the remnants of the bridge.

"Where are we going?" he asked.

"Do I have to tell you? Keep walking, and we'll get there."

We came to the spot where the Hitler Youth threw me into the river. "Do you remember?" I asked the Miller boy.

"Yes, but it wasn't me who threw you in the river."

"OK, so it wasn't you, but you were the leader of that gang. Climb on the railing." He did as he was told, and I punched him in the nose. He was bleeding. "Climb over," I told him. He climbed to the other side of the railing. "This is only the beginning. I know you can swim, so why don't you jump?" He held on to the railing, and I said, "Remember how you cut my hand?" Then I cut his hand and pushed him off the bridge. He sunk very deep and then came up and started to swim. I went back to the boat and took it to the west bank. I saw him way down by the bend in the river. I pulled the boat onto the bank and went toward Sossa's. On my way home, I felt my job was finished. "I'll let the other six goons go," I thought. "All I wanted was their leader."

As I continued back to Sossa's, I ran into Kestner's son, another boy who had done me a little wrong. Sometime before, when I was walking to Mike's, this boy was in his back yard by the gate. He had a rock hidden in his hand, and he threw it at me and hit me in the right shoulder. Then, he closed the gate and ran away. Now, I had the chance to get even. He was about eighteen years old. I stopped him and grabbed him by the shoulder. Then, I hit him right by the ear with the bayonet. He fell down, and I gave him a good kick in the ass. Then, I went home to Sossa's. I looked back, and he got up to go his own way.

That boy's father, Kestner, was also on my list. I had to get him now, before the war was over. He was the farmer who had chased me with the fork when I got into a fight with Sossa. So I went to see him one day. I went into his back yard, and he was home. He came out of the house, and we faced each other about a yard apart. I looked straight into his eyes, but he didn't want to look at me because he knew he was guilty. I said nothing. I just stared at him. He didn't have the guts to say anything, but he finally asked, "What do you want?"

I backed off a little bit from him.

"I came here for five liters of wine."

"What wine do I owe you?"

"Don't you remember?" I asked. "I saved a life for you! My own! For that good deed, you owe me five liters of wine." Right by the wall, I saw his pitchfork. I picked it up and said, "Some time ago, this fork was in your hands. Now, it's in mine. You jabbed me with this pitchfork. You could have killed me that day! True or not?"

Kestner looked me in the eyes. I scratched the fork on the stone, making sparks fly. "This day is my day!" I told him. "Since it's my day and I'm still living, you owe me five liters of good wine. If you think it's not true, remember the Nazis aren't here, the Americans are. You got it? You understand?"

He turned his gaze away. "That's true."

He led me to the cellar. I had my bayonet tucked in the back of my belt. There were many gallons of wine in the cellar. Kestner rinsed a bottle out, dried it with a towel, went to a barrel, opened up the valve, and filled the bottle with five liters of wine.

He corked it and said, "I am going to drink to you! I'm getting a glass for each of us, and we're going to toast to the new free world." We drank and toasted each other, and we laughed together. When we finished, I put my glass down on the table and said goodbye. He said, "Goodbye, Stanislaus."

I took the wine to my room. Guedraut saw me with the big bottle. "What have you got there?"

"A full bottle of wine," I said.

"Is that our wine from the hall?"

"No," I said. "Do you remember when Kestner chased me with the fork?"

"Yes, I remember that, and my father hit you with the hook, and you were bleeding."

"Today, Kestner felt sorry for me, and he brought me to his cellar, and we toasted and forgave everything that was between us. This was his present to me."

"That's nice of him," Guedraut said.

I was even with almost everyone who had given me trouble. I was going to forget about Thomas. He got his share because he got in trouble over the rifle and then was sick in the hospital for a long time. Thomas asked everybody where I was. He wanted to see me and asked why I didn't visit him in the hospital. I told everybody that I didn't want to visit because of the lousy deals with his cigarettes and his suit. I didn't want to see him again as long as I lived.

I also crossed Wasyl off my list. He evaporated. Nobody knew what happened to him. The only people left on my list were Alexander and Kessler. I'd have to wait to get them.

On May 8, 1945, the war with Germany was over. The German government had surrendered the day before, and the Americans put on a show of their strength for the German people. They put every plane they had into the air, crossing Germany to Berlin. I never saw so many planes in the air. They just kept coming, coming, coming. The German civilians were all surprised. It took an hour for all the planes to fly over. It marked the end of the war.

Hitler not only lost the war, but he lost his life. Everyone said it was a suicide.

I knew I would have to leave Schrcenau soon, and I might not get my chance to get even with Kessler and Alexander. The day didn't really look different from all the other days, but things were different. Not too long ago, we had a war. Now, it was all over.

A couple of days after the fly-over, I was working in the shed where we kept the wagon. It was about four o'clock in the afternoon. Sossa came to me and said, "You should leave here! Leave my house, and don't come back! The war is over. I don't need you anymore."

"The sun will be down soon," I said. "I can't go anywhere today. It'll be dark in a little while. Besides, I don't have the money to go anywhere. Why do I need to explain to you? You can't order me to do anything. I'm going to leave when I feel like it and when I want!"

He grabbed me like he always did. "You're going now! This minute!"

I pushed him away and punched him twice, once in the face. He fell under the wagon and was bleeding. I was bleeding, too. When he got up, I saw that I had knocked his two front teeth out. He went straight to his house. His wife screamed so everybody in the neighborhood could hear. Many of the neighbors came running into the back yard. There was Hans from across the alley and Miller, the father of the big boy. Miller had been waiting for a good time to get even with me for what I had done to his son.

I wasn't scared of anything. They were closing in on me, but I kept my cool, even though they were ready to beat me up.

"Don't come any closer," I said. "None of you!" I took the bayonet out from behind me. "You people tortured me so many times, and I'm still here. I almost died so many times, but I'm still alive — and I'm going to stay that way. I'm not joking. I'm ready to die right now in this back yard. But if I die, I'm taking one of you with me."

They stopped and listened to me.

"For two years, you people beat me up. You called Kessler and the mayor on me. Now, this is my time. Your time is ended. When will you understand the situation? Go home! This isn't Hitler's time anymore. The war is over!"

Miller said, "We're not going to wait until you kill us all!"

I backed off a little bit.

"About your son, Mr. Miller," I said angrily. "Did he tell you what he did to me? I'll bet he didn't tell you anything at all."

They knew the truth of what I said. The standoff ended as they went through the gate and back to their homes. Everything quieted down. Hans walked over to me and said, "Stanislaus, I'm not going to beat you up. I never intended to beat you up."

"I know. You were always nice to me, and I have nothing against you. I like you very much."

Then, he left.

So now all there was left to do was to go upstairs and pack my things, which were so few they could have fit in a cigar box. I left without any words. I didn't even see Guedraut, although she wasn't angry with me. That ended two years of hard work in Schrcenau.

The sunset had just begun when I went out Sossa's iron gate. I didn't know where to go, what I was going to eat, or where I was going to sleep. It looked as though I'd have to sleep in a field or a hay barn on this night. I couldn't go back to Sossa's now, and anyway, I had to leave there sooner or later.

"What have I done in these two years of hard work?" I asked myself. "I'm ashamed to go live in the street. Some people in this village like me, and some people don't. I should go back to Poland, but how am I going to get there? I have no money for a train or a plane? How can I show up at my parents' door with nothing?

What have I got to show for these years? What kind of money did I make? I'm at a bad pass.

"When I came from Poland, I had a little package with me and a loaf of bread for my trip. My father was beaten for giving it to me. I don't even have that package now. I have no good clothes or shoes, not even a single German mark for the trip. I haven't had supper this evening, and I don't know what I'm going to eat tomorrow. All this time in Germany was wasted! I earned nothing, and I learned nothing! I couldn't even go to school."

I was at a crossroads after my terrible young years. I wondered which road I should take. Which one was the right one? I thought that maybe I should find the American army, even though I was ashamed to beg for anything. The Americans were in Dettelbach, not very far away. I could easily walk up there, but I didn't know what I would say to them. I didn't know how to deal with soldiers.

Another problem was that it was already dark. I told myself, "At night, the Americans are standing guard, and they're not going to let me in anywhere. It's not going to work." I didn't see any way that anyone would help me. Maybe the Americans would come to Schrcenau, since they were moving back and forth so much. I shook my head and tried to think of a plan.

I was approaching the other end of the village, and decided to stop and say goodbye to my friend, Amelia, and the other Poles who had been working for Kessler and who had been staying on his farm since he disappeared. Then I thought, "How is that going to help me? To say goodbye and then leave?" I decided I would sleep in a hay barn overnight.

My heart still burned with the desire to get Kessler and Alexander, the last two on my list. I believed I would meet those thugs again someday.

𝔖eventeen

AMERICAN SOLDIER

I found a barn to sleep in, figuring I'd get a fresh start in the morning. I got up early the next day, and as I walked down the road, I ran into Mike, my Russian buddy.

"Where are you going?" I asked him.

"I'm just taking a walk," he said.

"Mike, I didn't have any supper or breakfast. Do you have anything to eat?"

We started walking toward the farm where he worked. When we got there, he said, "I have something for you to eat, and you can also sleep here. Don't worry. I have enough food here for both of us." We talked as I ate. Then, we went over by the river, and we kept on talking about our time in Schrcenau and what the future would bring. We went back to his room for lunch, and then we talked all the way over to the bridge. Mike wasn't working. Even the German civilians weren't working, except to feed the cows. It was like a holiday. Mike and I walked toward Kessler's. A group of French POWs was there standing by the gate. So were some of Kessler's foreign workers.

We all talked for a long time about what we were going to do and how we could get transportation back to our homes. We talked about how nobody had seen Kessler since the bridge was blown up. He didn't sleep at the house anymore, and nobody knew where he'd gone.

As we were talking, I noticed an American soldier standing in the main road with his helmet on and a rifle slung across his shoulder. When he noticed our group, he came toward us. He was a good-looking, big man in a clean, pressed uniform.

"Who are you people?" he asked.

"Me Polski," I said. "Stanislaus!" I pointed to Mike, "He Russian. His name's Mike. Nice to meet you."

We introduced him to the whole group, and we all talked happily. Eventually, Mike invited the soldier back to his room. We toasted each other and talked. The soldier gave us cigarettes, but I didn't take any because I didn't smoke. We were excited to be talking so freely. Besides English, the soldier spoke some German. We also spoke some French, which we learned from the POWs. We were speaking in a broken language, but we understood one another.

He asked if we could introduce him to some girls, if there were any girls in the village — a Fraulein or French girls or another nationality. He was just interested in meeting some girls. That's all he would talk about then.

Mike mentioned a place where a group of girls gathered.

"Mike, how do you know there are so many girls there?" I asked.

"Well, I know they get together in the evening and play games," he said. "I've heard about it and seen them go there."

The soldier was very interested in a place where a number of girls would be together.

It hit me that after a war, this could mean trouble. He had been through the war from beginning to end. I thought that this soldier had gone through hell, maybe worse than I had. He may not have seen a woman in years.

I spoke to Mike in Polish so the American wouldn't understand. "Mike, say no. Say you were kidding. Tell him there are no such girls over there."

"Yes, it's dangerous," Mike said. "Whatever will be, will be. I'm going to take him there. Are you coming with me?"

"I guess so," I said.

Mike started talking about what the German soldiers did during the war, raping women and sending them naked into the street. It happened everywhere the Germans invaded. "This guy went through hell, and all he wants is a woman," Mike said. "He probably hasn't seen a woman in years."

We started walking down the road. As we approached Sossa's tavern, Mike said, "Let's introduce him to Guedraut."

"No, Mike, no. You can't do this to me. Guedraut was good to me. You can't do that!"

"All right. We'll go over to the other girls' house." We headed toward a dead-end street near the Catholic cemetery. The house was right by the dead end. We walked through the gate, and Mike said, "Here's the door where the girls are. They should be upstairs."

The soldier knocked on the door with the butt of his rifle. No one answered. He knocked again. A farmer asked, "What do you want?"

The soldier said, "Open the door!"

"I'm not opening the door. I'm going to the police!"

There were no police around, so the soldier started knocking down the door. He slammed a board out and tried to reach through to open the lock. It wouldn't open. So he beat the rest of the door down. It was a strong door. When the soldier finally pushed it open, he fired a shot into the air to scare everyone inside. There was no light inside, so he found the switch and turned it on. He was the first one up the stairs. Mike followed, and I was last. In a bedroom upstairs, we saw through a half-open door that the girls were talking together. The soldier pushed the door completely open.

The girls were sitting on their beds, and it looked like they were ready to go to sleep. The soldier put the helmet on Mike's head and gave him the rifle to hold. He entered the room and closed the door. He was in there awhile. It looked as though he was picking the girl he wanted. The other six girls came out and went downstairs. After the soldier finished, he came out and said, "Get some of that if you want to, Mike. I'll be here watching the door!"

Mike said, "No, I don't want any."

"How about you, Stanislaus?" the soldier asked.

"No. I don't want anything."

So we went downstairs and walked out the broken door. We walked toward the main street. Then the

American soldier said goodbye and started going the way he had come. He had about five kilometers to his station in Dettelbach.

After the soldier left, Mike and I talked. We knew there would be trouble over this. Who was to blame? It was the soldier's fault that we took him there. If the Americans investigated, we would tell them what we did, but we didn't do anything wrong. The soldier asked us to be there.

I shook hands with Mike and said, "Goodbye, and tell the others who work at Kessler's goodbye for me because I won't see them again."

Mike wished me the best of luck on my journey. Then, he added, "I won't tell if you won't tell what happened up there. Please, don't say anything." Then, he said in Russian, "Goodbye, until I see you again." It was nice that he said that.

I started to go, and on my way, I passed Kessler's place. Everyone was sleeping. I was tired. There was nothing else to do but to sleep there. There was an extra board made into a bed, so that's where I slept that night. At about 10 a.m., Mike came over to say goodbye to these people for me, and there I was.

After I got dressed, some American soldiers and MPs walked right into Kessler's farm. One of them pointed to Mike and me, saying, "You two, come with me!" They put us on a jeep and took us to the priest's house. There were many trucks and jeeps around the house. There were many MPs there, too. We were being watched carefully, like real killers. We were taken upstairs to the living room and told to sit down in front of a table. Behind the table sat three American officers. They asked about what happened the night before.

The mother of the girl had gone on bicycle to tell the officers about the rape of her daughter. There were many papers on the table, probably all the complaints. In German, the officer asked us our names. Then, he asked, "Were you with an American soldier last night?"

I said, "Yes. We were together."

"Did he knock down a door to get into a house?"

"Yes."

"Why did you guys break down the door and walk into a strange house?"

"We didn't do anything. We were there because the soldier wanted us there," Mike answered. "Whatever the soldier told us to do, we did. I stood on the stairs with his rifle. Nothing else."

"What did the soldier do?" we were asked.

"He talked to the blond girl," I said.

"What did the soldier say?"

"He said he loved her, and that was all," I answered.

They continued to ask us questions. Some of them were about details I couldn't remember the answers to. The American officers looked very stern, as if we had killed everybody in the village.

Why did he care so much about this one girl? Why didn't he ask how many Germans raped women in the countries they occupied?

"How long did you know this soldier?" the officer asked.

I answered, "Last night was the first time we met."

"Did he harm you guys or the girl?"

"No, he didn't. He was a gentleman to us. He gave us candy and cigarettes. We took everything he gave but the cigarettes because we don't smoke."

"Stanislaus, do you think you could recognize him again?"

"No. I don't think so."

The American officer said, "You shouldn't have gone with the soldier."

"We didn't want to go," I said. "He almost forced us to show him where some girls lived."

"I'm going to bring a Polish man in to translate," the American officer said. I didn't know why. We seemed to be understanding one another in German. A Polish soldier came in to translate.

"The soldier and you two went against the law of the U.S. forces," he said.

I said, "No. We're not soldiers, and we didn't break any law."

"Stanislaus and Mike, do you feel you're guilty?"

I said, "No. We haven't done anything wrong." Mike answered the same way.

"But you two admit you were in the house with the soldier?"

"Yes. We were in the house, but we didn't hurt anybody," I said.

"Did you try to run from Schrcenau?"

"No," I said. "We were still here when you took us in."

"Where did the soldier go after you left the house?"

"To tell you the truth, we didn't know exactly where he came from or where he was going," I said.

The Polish soldier and the American spoke to one another in English.

"You two are going to jail," the officer told us through the translator. "You're not going to be beat up, but we're going to hold you until we have a suspect. Then, we're going to ask you and Mike if you recognize him. When you identify the suspect, you'll be released. But make sure it's the right man!"

"OK," Mike said. "If it's the right soldier, we'll tell you. Sir, I have something more to say. We didn't see what he did with the girl. They were by themselves in the room. We stood out on the stairs. He probably did the same thing German soldiers did across Europe. He was in the service five years, and he's only a human being. At least he didn't beat her up. She didn't scream. The Germans used to beat the women they raped, and sometimes killed them."

"That may be true," the officer said, "but we have a rule of law now. This isn't war time, and we Americans have to keep everything in order. We have to punish that soldier."

The interrogation was over. They took us downstairs and put us on a jeep. We were driven to Kitzingen. Because the bridge was down, we had to take another road to an out-of-the-way crossing. On our way, we saw many people out on the roads — foreigners, German civilians and soldiers, American soldiers riding in trucks. We saw French, Polish and Czech POWs, and truck after truck of Russian POWs. Traffic was heavy everywhere. Many people were celebrating.

The town of Kitzingen lay in rubble, but the jail was untouched. The jail was overloaded with prisoners — men and women. Mike and I were put into a room with twenty men. Our meal was much better than the Germans gave us. Still, I wouldn't recommend spending time there. Mike and I stayed in that cell overnight. Then, we asked the American supervisor if we could stay in the hall because the cell was so packed. We weren't killers or rapists. We did nothing wrong, so why should we suffer?

Mike and I decided that if we did recognize the soldier, we wouldn't identify him. We thought that if we did, it might put us in more hot water. We thought that we'd be considered guilty because we were with him, and maybe we'd be sent to jail for years, maybe even to hard labor. We asked ourselves many questions about the American law. Were they going to bring in the whole company or battalion and line them up so that the girl could identify the soldier? What if she picked an innocent man? How could she be sure who it was? They would probably shoot the wrong soldier. What did the big shots care anyway? What does the American government care? What does the American law care? These soldiers were just pawns, pushed like lambs to the slaughter in places like Normandy. What did that matter to the big shots? Even if the girl picked the right man, didn't he deserve some understanding? He'd been through hell. I don't think any European country would shoot a man for raping a woman, especially under these circumstances.

One day, at about two o'clock in the afternoon, they brought us outside to identify the suspect. By an iron gate stood three high-ranking officers and two translators — one Russian, the other Polish. Beside them was the suspect. They made us look and look and look.

They put the helmet on him and took it off. We both kept looking at him.

Through the translators, the officers asked, "Do you recognize this soldier?"

"No," I said. "I can't tell."

"How about you, Mike?"

"No. All soldiers look alike to me."

"Do you think this is the soldier who did it?"

We looked right into the soldier's eyes. He was very scared. We knew he was the one. We both said that he wasn't. The soldier's face relaxed.

The officers looked at us, then looked at the soldier. "You two young men said that this is not the soldier. Is that correct?"

"No. It's not the soldier. We really don't know him."

"Take another good look. Is this the soldier who was with you, Mike and Stanislaus?"

We answered simultaneously. "No, sir."

They put the soldier into a truck. The officers stood in a circle talking among themselves. Then, a colonel asked through the Polish translator, "Are you young men telling the truth?"

I answered, "Yes."

They asked Mike the same thing in Russian.

They moved away from us. We asked each other, "Why such a close investigation? We didn't kill anybody. The soldier didn't choke her to death. We saw her walk out."

"Mike, do you think they'll shoot the soldier?"

"That's a good question," he said. "Who knows what those crazy American officers will do to the soldier?"

"You're right, Mike. I just hope they don't shoot him."

Then, an American guard said, "That's all," and they took us into the hall. We sat on the bed and talked. All those officers with all their translators got nothing out of us.

Mike said, "That was a good idea to say we didn't know this soldier. Good for you, Stanislaus."

It wasn't too bad being in the hall. We ate at a table by the bed, and we could walk around. We could talk to the people in the cells, even the women.

We saw one of the American guards take a shine to one young woman. Sometimes, he'd talk to her for hours at a time. At one point, he let us out into the garden. We sat out there at an angle to the door, and we could see that young woman's cell. The American guard opened the cell door and went in.

We talked to each other in Polish. "We don't care what they're doing. We didn't turn in that other soldier, so why would we turn in this guard? Why should we? He treats us very well. He gave us a bed in the hall. It was nice of him. He didn't have to. He gave us cookies, candy, chocolates." What could we say? He was very good to us, and we'd never forget that.

Then, we started to count the days as our imprisonment dragged on. We were in there for ten weeks. I asked Mike, "Is this American justice? Innocent young boys held in jail for ten weeks for nothing? We didn't do anything. We didn't kill anybody. We didn't break down the door, and we didn't break the law. Oh, my God, Mike. I can't believe it's ten weeks, and we're still here."

We were soon told that we were being released. The guards opened the door for us and loaded two bags of candies, chewing gum, chocolates, apples, even cigarettes. As we were walking away, though, we wondered what good this stuff they gave us was. It wouldn't let us catch up with our lives, the ten weeks we'd lost.

As we walked, we saw the sky was more blue than it was before we went to jail. We saw that where there was no grass before we went in, now there were carpets of green grass.

We took deep breaths of the clean, fresh air, and we felt better already because we were free. "The sun is brighter than it was before all this happened," I said.

Mike answered in Russian, saying, "Everything's OK. We're going to live."

Eighteen

LIFE WITH AMERICANS

FROM the jail, we decided to go back to Schrcenau. We wanted to at least show ourselves so the villagers would know we're not the thugs they thought we were, that we weren't going to be in jail the rest of our lives.

About halfway back to Schrcenau, we saw a farmer working in a field on the right-hand side of the road. Beside him was a bicycle. We talked about how we could use that bicycle to get back to Schrcenau because it would be a long walk. Mike headed into the field toward the farmer, then the farmer held up the big iron hook he was working with and started running after Mike. Mike ran quickly toward me, and we both started running toward the road.

It was just as well that we didn't get that bicycle because when we got to the road, there was an American jeep going our way. We would have missed it had we taken the bicycle. We both smiled at our luck.

The jeep stopped. There were three Americans aboard, the driver, a lieutenant, and a sergeant.

My English had improved quickly over the past few months, and I said, "Welcome, Americans! I am Stanislaus and this is Mike."

The driver asked us, "Where are you going?"

The sergeant asked, "Who are you people? Are you German soldiers?"

"No," I answered. "We're not Germans. I am Polish, and Mike is Russian."

The sergeant then spoke in Polish. "Where are you coming from?"

"From Kitzingen. We were in jail there."

He asked, "Do you know any Nazis or SS officers?"

"We know some Nazis."

Then, they asked us to get in the jeep, and we climbed aboard.

The sergeant chuckled and asked, "Do you boys know a lot of Nazis?"

"Oh yeah! There's quite a few," I answered. Mike echoed my answer.

Then, Mike spoke in Polish, "You Americans think we are two Nazis."

The sergeant said, "No. We believe you. You're not Nazis."

Mike whispered to me in Polish, "Stanislaus. Don't make any jokes. They might arrest us and put us back in jail."

The sergeant said, "We won't hurt you. Don't worry."

The jeep continued almost to Dettelbach and then turned onto the road to Schrcenau. The bridge was still out, and we had to take a round-about route. Soon, we were approaching the village, near Kessler's farm. The jeep stopped by Kessler's house. The driver and the sergeant got out, while the lieutenant stayed with us. They went to the door and asked whether a Nazi named Kessler was there.

Whoever answered the door said, "There's nobody here by that name."

So the Americans came back to the jeep. They told us they were going to hunt down Kessler. The lieutenant asked if we would them find him because we knew what he looked like. We all took a walk around the grounds to see if there was any trace of him. Then, we got back in the jeep and headed down the main street toward the priest's house.

We were about halfway there when we saw the priest coming toward us. They stopped the jeep, and I spoke to the priest in German. "Father, do you know where Kessler is or where he might be?"

The priest had promised to help me hunt down Kessler before I went to jail.

He answered, "Yes. I know where he is. He's working in that field where the American bomber fell."

I said, "Thank you very much, Father."

I told the Polish sergeant where we had to go. We went up the hill and made a right turn onto a gravel road toward the field. As we neared the field, I saw him, sitting on a machine, raking hay. His workers were stacking it in big piles. I said to Mike, "God help me! That's him."

I told the sergeant, "That's him. That's the Nazi we came for."

The jeep stopped right away. The driver and the sergeant picked up their rifles and the lieutenant pulled out his pistol. Mike and I sat in the jeep. We said that Kessler must have thought that the heat was off, that the Americans wouldn't look for him anymore, that he was free as a bird.

The Americans trained their guns on him and called out, "Halt! Hands up!"

The lieutenant spoke to Kessler in German. They searched the Nazi and took away his pistol. They held his arm up and found his SS tattoo. Mike said, "That's what we were waiting for!"

We wanted to go out and draw some blood from Kessler ourselves, but we decided not to. It was enough that we fingered him for the Americans.

When they were done with him on the field, they sat him on the hood of the jeep, and we drove off down the road. We told the Americans all about Kessler. "That Nazi beat us up all the time for no reason. He often beat us until we were unconscious and bleeding. He killed a lot of war prisoners and sent some to concentration camps." Kessler didn't say a word. He just sat on the hood as we drove down the road.

I thought, "All the blood I lost and the hard work he stole from me — this is my chance to repay him." I hoped the American law would hang the devil.

We came to Dettelbach and turned Kessler over to the jail guards. The Americans said his actions would be investigated. It was hard to say what would happen, but we were sure that he'd get what he deserved. We were just happy to have helped put him in jail. I marked him off my list.

It was late in the afternoon when we arrived at the American army quarters in Dettelbach. The Americans were pleased to have caught a Nazi. The lieutenant asked us how many more we had on our list.

"There's some," I answered.

Meals were "chow time" in the American quarters. All the soldiers had a "mess kit" — a plate, spoon, knife, and fork — to bring along to the "mess hall." The lieutenant told Mike and me to get some supper. We were last in line, but even so, there was plenty of food in big containers. They filled our plates with chicken, potatoes, vegetables, bread, dessert peaches, coffee — whatever we wanted.

When we were finished eating, we took the jeep to the motor pool. We were taken to the supply room, and the Americans gave us new clothes — pants, shirt, jacket, boots, underwear, T-shirts and socks. We carried our new clothes to the shower room and put them down on a bench. When we stripped off our old clothes, we threw them in the garbage, shoes and all. We showered and happily put on the new clothes.

When we were done, the lieutenant came to see us. "Tomorrow morning, you're going to get breakfast, and sometime after that, we're going to another town to hunt for Nazis. Could you come with us and show us where they are?"

Of course, we answered yes.

"Where do we sleep?" I asked.

"That won't be a problem," the lieutenant said. "We've got plenty of blankets, pillows and cots. We'll set you in the kitchen hall for the time being. Maybe later, we can find you better quarters."

We felt very good after our showers and the good meal. The sergeant came to us and asked if we needed blankets, towels, and soap. We did. So he took us to the supply room and gave us what we needed. We thanked God we were in good hands. The sergeant took us to the sleeping quarters. It was a big hall that looked like an old courtroom to me. We were going to bunk here with the sergeant and about twenty other men. He said there were no extra cots or pillows right then and we'd all have to sleep on the floor. The sergeant went about busily straightening things out for the soldiers and us.

All the soldiers had plenty of questions for us about our experiences in the war. We answered the best we could. The conversation lasted for a couple of hours before lights out. We made ourselves as comfortable as we could on the floor. We put blankets on top of rolled-up raincoats to use as pillows. For the time being, this would be a good place to sleep.

In the morning, we had breakfast and straightened up the sleeping area before the lieutenant came to take us out hunting Nazis again. We caught one before lunch and another two in the afternoon. They were all the Nazis we knew about. In thanks, the Americans offered us jobs. Before supper, the sergeant said, "I'll show you two where you're going to work." He took us to the motor pool and introduced us to the mechanics and the staff sergeant there.

We reported to the motor pool right after breakfast the next morning. The staff sergeant introduced us to all the vehicles — the jeeps, the half-ton trucks, the two-ton trucks. He showed us a hitch and how it worked. We started out changing and repairing tires. He showed us how to change the oil and the barrel where we were to get rid of the old oil.

After working for a while, the lieutenant came in and asked Mike to go with him. The lieutenant gave Mike a job as his attendant. I wasn't jealous. I liked my job in the motor pool. Workers of many nationalities were there. I liked the job, and, more important, I knew I'd get a good meal for it.

The lieutenant came by and watched me for a while. When he saw I'd finished one job, he asked, "Do you like working in the motor pool? If you like it, you'll be with us for quite a while."

"I like my job very much, and I want to stay," I answered.

So Mike got to do his job, and I did mine. We were separated now, but we got to see each other once in a while.

A couple of days later, the lieutenant came to speak to me again. "I'm glad you like the job, but right now, I don't know how I'm going to pay you for the work. I know I'll be able to work out some pay for you in the future, but I don't know how long it will take."

"I don't want any pay or money right now. You people feed me, and that's good enough. I like working in the motor pool very much, sir."

"Very good," he said.

All this time, the war with Japan continued. The soldiers were worried about possibly being shipped over there. For many of them, the fight with Germany had been enough. As one soldier said, "If we go, we go. What can we do?"

Fortunately, good news came quickly. First, word came that Russia had declared war on Japan. Then, on August 6, we heard that the atom bomb had been dropped on the Japanese city of Hiroshima. Despite the destruction and the many deaths this single bomb caused, the Japanese wouldn't surrender. On August 9, the Americans dropped an atom bomb on Nagasaki. The Japanese finally saw that resisting such a destructive force was impossible. A few bombs could destroy all their major cities. Japan surrendered on August 15. The war was over.

That meant more changes. Our company soon merged with the First Infantry Division. The old-timers in our company weren't happy about the merger because there were new people to deal with and things were run differently. We had to make new friends. I didn't really care. I still had the job as a mechanic, and it gave me the opportunity to get to know many of the soldiers. Many became good friends. A number of them could speak other languages, including Polish and Russian.

These new soldiers had come from the front. They had a lot of experience in life, and they went through hell in the war. They were good to me, like brothers. We spent a lot of time together, working and going into town. We'd go to chow together and get doughnuts and coffee at the PX. We all slept in the big hall, too. By now, things were getting comfortable. We all had cots.

Everything was fun and interesting to me. They started to pay me for my work. It was good pay. I had meals, a good bed, and lots of friends. I even went to visit Rita in Schrcenau every once in a while. I was very satisfied with my life now.

Rita's mother, her name was Fauks, was in sad shape. She had lost both her husband and her son, Joe, my friend, in the war. She had been a widow for many months. I felt sorry for her, and one day, I introduced her to an older soldier. After a while, Rita's mother came alive again. She started to look younger and happier. She got a job taking in laundry from the soldiers and me. She was paid well. This was a happy time for Rita's mother, as well as the rest of us. We went swimming together in the Main. In the evening, we'd get together and play cards, and the soldier brought beer. We laughed and talked and had lots of fun.

With the war over, though, things changed quickly. Some of the old soldiers from the front line started going home to the U.S. Some were transferred to different towns and groups. I was with a group that was transferred to Wurzburg. That made it a twenty-five-kilometer trip to see Rita in Schrcenau. While I was in Wurzburg, I still visited her often. Rita suggested that maybe we could get married.

"I'm sorry, Rita," I told her. "I have a good job with the soldiers, but I don't make enough to get married. Besides, I'm a little young yet. Let's wait and see what happens."

Soon after, the entire company I was with shipped back home to the States. All except for the driver, the sergeant, and the lieutenant that Mike and I met the day we got out of jail. All of us, including Mike, went to Nuremberg, where we were attached to the First

Battalion. I still had the same job fixing jeeps and trucks. By this time, I could clean carburetors, grease and pack the front bearings, and install mufflers, as well as change tires. I'd even go for gasoline at a depot across Nuremberg.

One day, Corporal Kelley, whom I worked for, decided I would test a jeep with him.

"Stanislaus, jump in the jeep, and you drive this time," he said.

We began to drive around a big factory that was on a rail spur. I took things too slowly for Kelley.

"Why are you driving so slow? We're not in town. There's nobody here to give you a ticket. Step on the gas. Let's get some speed to test out the jeep. That's what we're here for."

So I stomped down on the gas pedal, and the jeep took off.

"Boy! We're going now!" Kelley said. He added that the jeep seemed to be working fine now.

"Which way should I go?"

"That way!" Kelley said, pointing to the right.

All of a sudden, he yelled, "Stop! Stop! Stop! There's a big hole."

I slammed the brakes, stopping just inches from the edge.

"How the hell did you do that?" Kelley asked. "I'll bet you couldn't do that again."

We jumped off the jeep to check things out.

Kelley whistled.

"Holy shit! That was close."

The jeep's bumper was hanging over the hole.

What we didn't know beforehand was that there had been a turntable to turn around the freight trains that loaded and unloaded at this factory. During the war, however, the rails and turntable were taken out, leaving this huge hole.

Kelley told everyone at the motor pool about our wild ride, telling them what a good driver I was. We had a lot of laughs and drove together many times after that.

I adapted to this new town, with its different style and atmosphere. Nuremberg and Furth were twin cities. The Allies had not bombed Furth, however, because it was a Jewish city. Nuremberg was bombed, of course. Rubble was everywhere. It was hard to believe that among that rubble, you could find a lot of restaurants and places to dance. You could dance and eat in almost any part of town. You could even go to the movies. Furth was just as alive, and there was no rubble.

I got to know some old Germans who hadn't been in the army. They would invite me to their houses, and we'd eat and drink. I'd usually bring some food and beer. Another Polish man named Marian Kowalski also started hanging around with this circle of Germans. We had a really good time. Some of the Germans were musicians in a band, and they took us along when they played in different halls. The band included a bass, drums, piano, and button accordion. We sure had a ball. There were lots of girls to dance with and good music.

One of these Germans worked pressing clothes for the American company I was in. I had an accordion that I dragged around with me to practice whenever I had a chance. He asked me if he could buy it from me. He played my accordion so well that I gave it to him.

I said, "You press my clothes and take us to dances, so take this as my gift."

I went to Schrcenau one last time to see Rita. I found out that Rita's mother had married the American soldier, and he was going to take her to America. Rita's mother was so happy that she thanked me. So did the soldier.

The bridge over the Main had been repaired. Tears started to well in my eyes as I thought about Alexander, Sossa's son. I wouldn't be back in Schrcenau again. I would never get my revenge on him.

I went back to Nuremberg, where my life was pretty good, and I had no complaints.

Young girls were as plentiful as fish, and you could catch them with the right bait. Some of these girls would go out with Americans and then rob them. Some of these girls would marry Americans. Other girls liked the foreigners better. These Europeans were from all over — Poland, Czechoslovakia, Romania, Estonia, Latvia, Lithuania, France, Belgium, Italy. There were even some young British men who came to look at the Dachau concentration camp, miles to the south. I also went with some of these girls. Fortunately, no one robbed me or harmed me, day or night.

Sometimes, we'd go with the American soldiers to the river in summer. There were so many people there, it was a lot of fun. Sometimes, the Germans would be angry that the women were going out with the soldiers and foreigners. Then, there'd be a fight. I almost got in a fight, but the girls we were with didn't care what the German men were saying.

You couldn't blame the girls. They liked the money we spent on them. For the Germans, times were tough. There was a shortage of just about everything, including fun. The girls liked us because we always had something for them, and we could take them to dances. Some of these girls were lucky if they had one potato to boil at home.

The German men started stealing from the Americans whatever they could, just to make a few bucks. The Germans would steal suitcases in the railroad station and put the blame on foreigners.

One day when I was at the railroad station with my friend, Marian, we caught a small boy stealing like crazy. It happened in the afternoon, in broad daylight. We stopped the boy and noticed he had a Polish eagle on his chest. We tried to talk with him in Polish, but he only understood German. So many of these young German thieves wore the emblems of different countries. It was a good cover. It allowed the German government to cry that the foreigners were responsible for all the crime going on.

We took the boy out of town by streetcar and went to a park to question him. He told us that there was grown-up German who organized this type of crime.

"Is your father in this gang, too?" I asked.

"Yes," he said.

Marian told me in Polish, "I'm going to slap him a few times so he'll go home and tell his father that somebody caught him and he doesn't want to do this anymore."

Marian slapped him a few times, and he was going to hit him some more, when I stopped him.

"Marian, stop that right now. He's only a small boy. He's just fifteen. He did what his father told him to do, that's all. He's innocent. Marian, you must understand, I was in the same position when the Nazis beat me up all the time for nothing. You don't know what it's like. You're twenty-three years old. Have some understanding. You can't kill this boy just because he's German. It's a very bad time. Everybody's hungry. There's hardly any food. That's why they're doing this. So let him go, Marian. Let's not worry about this."

Marian released him, and we put him on a streetcar so he could go wherever he wanted.

I told Marian, "This kind of thing is happening all over Germany. Believe me, we can't do anything about it."

At the First Infantry Division, everything was changing. Old soldiers were shipping out, going home to the U.S. The replacements who came in from the States didn't know anything about the war, and they didn't understand life here. They did no work. They just loafed and gave everyone trouble. These soldiers would just wait for chow time, and then after chow, they'd go out with the German girls. The girls were waiting at the gate by the dozens.

These soldiers wouldn't just take the girls out to a movie or a restaurant. They'd load little bags with all kinds of food from the kitchen and things like chocolate and cigarettes, and give them to the girls. This caused a shortage in the mess hall. Food had to be rationed for the company of soldiers and foreign workers. All that was left was bread and beans. The mess sergeant ordered more food, but it happened

220

again. No more coffee. No more sugar. No more good
stuff to eat.

This kind of American soldier hated the foreign
workers. All they did was steal and chase girls. I saw
some of these soldiers give their rings and watches
away. They even gave away 45-caliber pistols, which
the Germans all wanted, to the girls.

This was happening all over Germany, wherever the
occupation troops were.

Everything was being stolen. A pair of American
transportation companies in Nuremberg stole all the
mess hall food and sold the goods like coffee and sugar
to Germans on the black market. They stole cans of
gasoline by the hundreds, trailers, tires, even jeeps and
trucks, and sold all of these things to Germans. The
Germans would paint the military vehicles in other
colors to keep them.

The colonel then ordered guards placed everywhere,
twenty-four hours a day. That calmed down some of
the thievery.

The First Infantry moved again. This time to Munich.
Things were pretty much as they were in Nuremberg. The
young soldiers coming in from the U.S. were very evil.
They would come to German taverns and dance halls
and make a lot of trouble. They started to fight and push
women around if they wouldn't go with them. They all
picked on foreigners, too. These Americans would hit or
kick the foreigners for no reason. They'd give the
foreigners extra hours of work and wouldn't pay them for
it. There was no hot water for the showers, so they sent
the foreigners to chop wood to heat the water. If the
foreigners refused, they'd be kicked or beaten.

Mike and I still stayed in Nuremberg with the old First Infantry. We numbered about one hundred twenty men, with the officers and the motor pool. Even there, the new soldiers made things worse. Then, the Americans stopped paying us foreigners in military scrip. They started paying us in German Marks, which were worthless. We didn't have Sundays or Saturdays off anymore. We worked seven days a week. The foreigners had to get wood for the stove so the soldiers could keep warm in the house, even though it was September and just a touch cool. These guys acted like kings. They did nothing!

On weekends, they had girls in the barracks. Almost all of the girls were naked. A Serb civilian told me that it happened every Saturday and Sunday.

They also got on me. Across the street, there was a bar and dance hall. They heard me play the accordion and dragged me over to the saloon. They wanted me to play for them. I tried to get out of it by saying I couldn't play dance music, but they said they'd heard me playing in my room. So I played for them. It started at seven o'clock and I played till ten. I hardly got any breaks. They danced with all the women, and they gave me a beer for my trouble.

The new motor pool sergeant was a devil, too. A couple of Germans had been working in the motor pool about a week or two when they didn't report for work. It was a German holiday and they had taken off. When they came back the next day, they had me translate for them so they could tell the sergeant why they hadn't come in.

The motor pool sergeant said, "We don't observe any German holidays over here. We don't even observe our

American holidays. Stanislaus, tell them they're fired. Tell them to go home." I told them.

A few days after that, the company moved out. I didn't go with them. Mike shipped out with the lieutenant, though. A new company came in, and I had a chance to get a job in the kitchen as a cook's helper. The mess sergeant was pleased with my work, and the first cook liked me, too. We cooked and put food on the soldiers' plates, and everything went pretty well.

A week later, more foreign workers were hired. They hired my friend Marian Kowalski and some Latvians and Lithuanians. About ninety percent of the new employees were Estonians. I became the first cook, and they gave me some helpers. Kowalski was the fire man for the stoves. He kept the stoves running. An Estonian did the hiring and firing. We had many workers to clean everything in the house, even the big hall. They hired people for PX work and hired guards for the PX. Many of these guards were Estonians, as were some of the kitchen workers and the cleaners.

I found out about the politics of these hirings from an Estonian kitchen worker. One day he asked, "Do you know how I can get rid of this?" And he raised his arm to show me an SS tattoo. A number of Estonians had volunteered for the Nazi SS. The Estonian SS officers were even more feared than the Germans. They were vicious men who worked as guards in the concentration camps and at the camps where foreign workers were dispatched to hard labor.

"I don't know how to take that off," I said. "You probably need a plastic surgeon." Then, I asked, "Are there any more like you here?"

"Oh, yes, indeed," he said. "The new American colonel is of Estonian blood, that's why he hired so many Estonians. He doesn't check, he just hires us."

Things went well for a while. The soldiers did their work and marched and exercised as well.

Later, it came out that the people who worked at the PX were stealing. The guards must have been keeping quiet about it, too. The stolen goods were turning up on the black market. I found out later through my helpers that the PX guards were all SS men, and that there were two SS men working in the kitchen.

One time, I sat in my room alone and began to think. "Should I go back to Poland? Back to my parents?" I was looking over my papers and photographs, which included pictures of American soldiers and officers. I said to myself, "If I go back to Poland, I'll have to get rid of these. Pictures like this could get me sent to Siberia when I try to cross the border. Poland's not free now. I don't want to live under Stalin's rule." It was the same as in 1939, when Hitler took half of Poland. The Russians were doing the same things, raping women, killing people, and robbing them.

Marian Kowalski had come from Warsaw to work here. So I asked him how things were in Poland now. "Let me get this through your head, Stanislaus. You'd better get the idea of going back to your parents out of your mind. It's no better than in 1939." He put his hand on my shoulder. "No, no, no. You don't want to go back. You've got a good job here, so stick around and stay alive."

In time, more American soldiers and officers came to this company, and the kitchen was overcrowded. So they set up a second kitchen. I was transferred to the new kitchen as first cook. This kitchen was just for the American soldiers and officers. The old kitchen served the civilians who worked for the company.

Pretty soon, the whole support community for the company was taken over by Estonians. They set up an Estonian kitchen hall for the workers. They had a special band on weekends, and there was beer and dancing. An American couldn't go into their area, even though it was paid for the by the U.S. government. The company colonel married an Estonian woman, and the Estonians had more power. Many were hired, even though they weren't needed. The colonel's stepdaughter married an American lieutenant.

Things got so bad that some Americans complained about the Estonian kitchen being run as a dance hall on U.S. money. So the Estonians rented a hall about two blocks away, and everything continued as it had. Even Estonians who weren't working for the company could go in and get a beer.

Kowalski and I walked over to the Estonian dance hall one Saturday night after work. Being civilians, we were allowed in. We wanted to do a little dancing and drink a bit. We sat down at a table and ordered a beer.

An Estonian civilian who worked in the Estonian kitchen came over to us and said, "Stanislaus, somebody outside wants to see you." So I went outside, and the man who'd showed me his SS tattoo was there. I had seen a few of the other old SS men talking to each other a few yards away, so I was suspicious. "Did you want to talk to me?"

"Stanislaus. You work in the American kitchen?"
"Yes."

The SS man said, "Oh. I made a mistake. The suit you are wearing. I made a mistake. Go back in. I'm sorry."

I returned to our table, and Kowalski asked me, "Who called you out?"

"You know the other guy in the civilian kitchen?"

He said, "Oh, that guy!"

"There's something funny going on," I said. "Maybe they're drunk."

Then, the same guy came in and said there was a Polish man who wanted to see Kowalski outside. I sat for quite some time, then I got myself a beer and another one for Kowalski. I put them on the table. I just sat there and drank my beer. When I finished it, I thought, "I'd better go out and see what happened." No one was outside. I went back in and drank the beer I'd bought for Kowalski. I figured he wasn't coming back in any time soon. Anyway, I could buy him another when he got back.

When I finished, I decided to go by Kowalski's apartment. He was living in Furth near some older Germans we knew. I knocked and asked if Kowalski was home. The woman of the house answered, "He's not here yet. Wasn't he with you?"

"He was," I said, "but I haven't seen him for a while. We were having a beer at the dance hall, and someone asked him to go outside. I haven't seen him since then. I thought maybe he came here."

Because it was already dark, I didn't think I'd have much luck hunting for him, so I headed home. I wondered what could have happened to him. I was worried. It was early yet, so I didn't want to go to sleep.

I started thinking about those SS men standing outside the dance hall. Maybe they didn't like him. Maybe they killed him. I was pretty sure that if he was all right, Marian would come visit me to say where he'd been. I thought I might as well go back to the dance hall and see if I could find the SS man I talked to. He wasn't there. Neither were any of the others. So I went back home. I decided to be very careful and took a longer route home. I wanted to be safe because I thought I'd probably be next.

Two days later, I opened the paper to find a story that a man had been beaten to death in an alley. The man's identification had been stolen, and the police weren't sure who the victim was. There was a photograph, and it was Kowalski. I went to Kowalski's apartment and knocked on the door. I asked the old Germans, "Did you see the paper today?"

"No. Not yet."

So I showed them the article and the picture.

"My God! It's Marian Kowalski!"

I went to the colonel and talked to him about it.

"What was the man's name?" he asked.

"Marian Kowalski," I said.

"Yes," he said. "I know him. He was the fire man in the American kitchen. He was a nice young man. It's hard to believe he was killed."

"Yes. He was beaten to death in an alley!"

"That's a shame," he said, "but who could have killed him?"

"Well, there are some people working here who used to work for the SS. Some of them even showed me their SS tattoos."

"You mean, working here, for this company?"

"Yes, sir."

"I'll have my officers check into this." Then, he said, "Stanislaus, you're working as the first cook in the American kitchen, aren't you?"

"Yes, sir!"

"You're doing a wonderful job," he said. "Listen, Stanislaus. I'll let you know when I find out something about Marian. Are you and Marian related?"

"No," I said. "I'm just his friend."

The investigation went nowhere. Nobody could find out who killed Kowalski.

I quit my job in the American kitchen because of what I had told the colonel. I was afraid it would get around. I didn't want to tangle with the Estonian SS.

𝔑ineteen

WHEN I quit my job, I stayed the night with the old German folks in Furth. I had put myself in a difficult position. I didn't have much money. It would run out pretty quickly if I rented an apartment and had to buy meals. What could I do? I was just sixteen years old, and I didn't have my parents to help me or give advice. There was no one to turn to, and I couldn't go back to Poland with Stalin in power. Working for the Germans was out of the question. They had no work themselves, and now the German civilians were starting to put their noses in the air and saying that foreigners should go home. They knew very well that with the Americans there, they were in good hands. They could say what they wanted and act as they pleased. We never heard them say we should go home in wartime, when they captured us and brought us here to work at hard labor.

A man's youth decides what he will become. It determines everything he will know and what decisions he'll make for his life.

For me, at this point, there were only two ways to go: school or the army. Which would I choose? I didn't have money for school. I heard about a school in Regensburg where a Polish organization gave you a fair deal to go but not very much money. Meanwhile, the Polish Second Corps was forming new guard companies in Mannheim and Kieferthal.

I took the train to Regensburg and tried the school first. I thought I would learn something there, but within a week, I could see that I couldn't concentrate on my studies. I couldn't remember anything I was being taught. If I thought hard, I got dizzy. The change from my past few years of life was too great, so I had to quit school.

So, I got on the train to Mannheim and registered with the guard company. A Polish lawyer I knew in Nuremberg had given me guidance. He thought this would be the best thing for me after I quit working for the Americans. He wrote a letter on my behalf to the Polish officers in Mannheim. That letter helped me a lot.

The Polish guards issued me a black uniform with a patch of silver wings. The Polish guards had taken over a big facility in Mannheim. We used a large sports field for exercises and marching. We even sang as we marched. We met with the officers every day, and they trained us to use rifles and fighting techniques. About three platoons had previous experience with rifles and marching. Physically, I felt very good. Although I was tired from exercising and marching, I didn't have any dizzy spells. An officer asked me, "How come you hold your head down?"

"I had an accident and have had trouble with my neck ever since," I told him.

He softened a bit and offered some compassionate advice, "Try to hold it straight to strengthen your neck muscles, and you'll come out of it."

After two months of hard exercise, my platoon was sent to Dachau.

We shipped into Dachau by train. At the station, a Polish sergeant and lieutenant awaited us. American trucks took us to our barracks. These had been the concentration camp's German barracks during the war. Camp Dachau was very big and very clean. It was landscaped with flowers and trees, and a small creek ran through. There was also fairly large man-made lake. There were three high-dive boards, stacked above one another. The German guards would swim and dive there.

There was also something very unclean here. The ovens where the Germans destroyed people stood there just as they had during the war. You could see a pile of bones and ashes from the people. I was standing on the ashes and bone fragments of real people. During the war, millions died and were burned. Very few came out alive. Now, I was walking on these camp roads, the same roads where people had fallen and died of starvation. I was finally seeing Dachau, where I would have been deported for hard labor in 1944 if not for the Austrian policeman. I thanked that Austrian policeman for saving me from this. "My God! I'd be laying in that pile of bones if not for that officer. Now, I'm a guard here, making sure the Nazis don't escape. How about that?"

We looked at the huge ovens, and we saw the gas chambers, big cement halls that the Germans filled with people and then filled with gas. I saw the places where they tortured people, and blood was spattered all over the walls. We saw piles of skulls, tiny and big.

I didn't know how anybody else felt, but for me, seeing all this was terrible. I shook like a leaf. I almost vomited. For two days, I couldn't eat. I thought all the dead were passing through my food.

After a few days, the platoon rested. They gave us a talk about the camp policy.

"We are the guards, and we're guarding many barracks of German Nazi prisoners. These prisoners are not the highest-ranked like Goering and Himmler, but they are pretty high Nazi officers. They are responsible for all these dead people. You must always be alert guarding them. We've already had incidents when we took them from the barracks to trial. They've jumped guards and choked them. I repeat, you must be alert all the time, with every step you take."

At Camp Dachau, we had seven Polish companies, a battalion, and two platoons of cavalry. The cavalry patrolled the perimeter fence on horseback. The company I was in escorted the Nazis from the barracks at Camp Dachau to the court. The court was made up of officers from the Allied powers. Most of them were Americans.

Another company guarded the camp's gates, monitoring who entered and left. Other companies guarded the seven barracks. The barracks held doctors who experimented on people, concentration camp personnel, war pilots, and many others who engaged in the cruelty of Germany's war.

Camp Dachau also held about 5,000 other prisoners of war and civilians. Many of the German prisoners were driven out to the forest to cut trees, and they were guarded by the Polish guards. There were also at least two companies of American soldiers in the camp, living in a big apartment building. The American soldiers guarded the gates with the Polish guards, exchanging shifts. A number of American civilian women worked in the camp offices.

Before the war, Dachau was small, like the villages I worked in. Now, the town had grown, with four- and five-story buildings in some places.

The barracks were built well, and they were comfortable. We talked about sports. There was a small Olympic field where we could play soccer, American football, baseball. We could golf and swim, too. There were contests for the fastest swimmer and the best divers. If you wanted to meet a beautiful English or American girl, the place to go was the horse trails. A major of the Polish guards owned the horses and was pleased to let anyone ride, especially the American and civilian women. To ride the horses was a good sport, and there were plenty of girls to date there.

How sweet it was to be guarding the Nazis in court. I was the guard who escorted Otto Skorzeny to the court and stood guard over him inside. Skorzeny was about six feet, six inches tall with a big frame. They said he had invented a gun that killed instantly with poison bullets. Skorzeny also rescued Benito Mussolini from captivity in the Abbruzzi mountains after the Fascist Party disbanded and the Allies were set to invade Italy. Skorzeny would never escape from Dachau while I guarded him.

I listened to the judges describe the ugly deeds these prisoners did in wartime — from shooting down parachutists to making gloves from human skin to forcing foreign women to have sex with German shepherd dogs. There were many international witnesses there to identify these killers.

They had special halls where they lined up the Nazis so people could pick them out. I was even asked if there was anyone I could identify. I looked for Kessler, but he wasn't there. People came from thousands of miles around to see these thugs and point the finger at them.

I talked to a few of these accusers, and they told me the terrible things the prisoners did. Many of them asked where Eichmann was. Did anyone know where he was hiding? Some of these prisoners may have killed millions of people.

You had to show a pass at the gate to get in or out of camp. Going through the gate, everything had to be checked. Guards inspected the jeeps and vehicles coming in and out.

Unbelievably, some German Nazis who were released stayed in town and attacked American soldiers at night. They also began to attack Polish guards. A lot of Americans and Poles were beaten up on the streets of that small town, some were even shot. The top Polish and American officers at the camp decided to deal with this by ordering that every American be accompanied by a Polish guard when he left camp. If three Americans were going out, two Polish guards would have to go with them. The Germans were afraid of us. We carried concealed weapons. Some of us carried M1 carbines under our black coats. The trouble with the Germans soon ended. Many of them were scared away, and some were shot.

We had good reason to want to go to town safely. There were a lot of dances on the weekend, and sometimes even on Wednesday night. A group of Polish guards formed an excellent band with violin, trumpet, saxophone, piano, and clarinet. There were many girls to dance with. There was a snack bar and beer. And we got along well, the Polish and the Americans. English and American girls came to these dances too. Some came in from Munich and other surrounding towns. Lots of officers brought girls, too. The girls were so pleased to go with the Americans or us guards. Civilian wives came without their husbands when they had an argument.

Everybody almost forgot that there had been a war between us.

In camp, it was hard to forget, though. German prisoners tried to escape. Some were captured. Some were killed. Some did escape. You could see women prisoners flirting with the soldiers. There was a tunnel between the men's and women's prison barracks. This wasn't allowed, and when the camp command found out, the tunnel was closed with cement.

A prisoner managed to make a hole through the hall of one bunker. He got out of his cell and across the yard but was caught as he tried to go over the barbed wire.

Many prisoners cut their wrists because they didn't want to go to court. Some were saved. The camp command decided to put a barber shop in the hallway so the prisoners wouldn't need or get hold of razor blades. One Nazi woman got pregnant, even though she was in solitary confinement. Everyone thought the father was the American doctor, the only man to visit her in confinement. Nobody knew for sure.

The hearings came to an end after a year. Many of the Nazis were transported to Ludwigsburg. I translated English, Polish and German for the officers at this time. I was with the officers constantly and felt honored to have this duty. We Polish guards marched these 2,000 Nazi prisoners to a freight train, where they were locked up in boxcars. Security was tight. Two platoons of Polish guards and an American officer got aboard to watch the prisoners. Each time the freight train would stop in a town along the route, we had to get out and make sure that all the doors were still locked.

When we got to Ludwigsburg, we Polish guards and the American officer got out. We surrounded the train. Each Polish guard put a bullet into the barrel of his M1 rifle, ready to fire. The American officer was ready with his machine gun. Then, we opened the boxcar doors, ordered the Nazis out, and told them to form a line. We marched them down the main street of Ludwigsburg, through the middle of the big town. German civilians lined up along the street and watched, like this was a parade. At the end of the route, we left the Nazis in the

Ludwigsburg jail. Then, we took a passenger train back to Dachau.

Another group was released from Dachau, and a group of Americans took them almost to the Russian occupation zone.

On May 3, we Polish people celebrated a major holiday. The Polish major and the American colonel and their staffs put together a big parade. The celebration began with a Mass, held in a field where all seven Polish companies gathered. Three priests said the Mass. When they raised the Eucharist, we presented our rifles, put them down, and stood at attention for three minutes. Then we took the rifles and slung them back on our shoulders. After Mass, we marched to the sound of a band, and displayed the Polish and American flags. Civilians gathered along our route. As we passed the reviewing stand where the Polish and American officers stood, the members of each company turned their heads in unison, facing the officers. We held them that way until the whole company passed.

Two weeks later, all the companies were moved to new posts. Two Polish companies went to France. I was sorry I didn't ship out with them. I had the chance. I was picked to work in a special platoon that functioned like the MPs, but that only lasted a month. They moved my platoon, and we had to drive trucks to our Munich post — Alabama Company. We had to guard a big barbed-wire fence outside buildings where American GI uniforms were stored. We did it in four-hour shifts.

Our company performed well, so they gave us a lot of recreation — a pool table, ping pong table, chess, playing cards, and exercise machines. There was also a hall where shows were held. Comedians appeared there, as did a Polish singing group called the Happy Fours. Civilians came to these events, too.

In the winter, a field was flooded to make an ice rink. I found a pair of ice skates and had a good time. Others from my platoon saw me skating, and after about three days, the guys from the platoon, including some officers, worked up the courage to join me.

A short while after that, we got new leadership — an American captain named Duman and a Polish captain named Olecha.

Duman changed everything on his first day. There were no more shows, no more dances, no more recreational items (he must have sold them). Everybody said he was a mad dog. He was an impossible man. I'd say he was completely nuts, and whoever gave him the rank of captain must have had a problem, too. Duman gave the Polish officers a hard time, too.

Captain Duman cut our meals. The meals we did get made us sick. Many of us, including me, developed jaundice. Under Duman, we not only had guard duty but hard labor. He screamed at us worse than the SS. We had to pay for our uniforms. It was impossible to tolerate that man. He was living in a private home owned by some Germans, and at certain hours, he told us to dig a basement under the German building.

We'd all just about had it. I could probably get release papers and get out of there, but there were no other prospects for making money — except the black market. The black market was illegal, but those who weren't afraid to die or go to jail could make money.

I had to go to a private doctor to treat my jaundice. The doctor told me to buy a bunch of apples, peel them, and cook them into apple sauce. I did what the doctor said, but I had to do it under cover so that the captain and his crew didn't find out. The doctor also prescribed some pills. Everybody else had to do the same for himself. So, it was very important for me to keep the job for a few more weeks, until I got well.

When I got well, I didn't have much money. I was just about broke, in fact. I gained some weight. One of my friends said that I looked very well after having been so sick. At that point, I didn't care what happened to me. When I felt stronger, I entered the black market. You could get many years in jail for being in the black market. It didn't take any education to work the black market. The only hard part was making sure the American or German police didn't catch you.

I was the first in our platoon to enter the black market. I had good connections with buyers, the people I got my merchandise from. The buyers were two Jews and a German. They had cars, and they'd go anywhere to sell their wares. Sometimes, they even went to the Russian-occupied zone. In a short while, one of my friends, Masterniak, joined me in my work. Masterniak owned a pistol, which he never fired. He just used it to scare customers who were late in paying. We didn't have to use weapons on everyone. If we knew a man well, we might even help him.

The black market brought us enough money to live on. I even bought a new suit and some civilian clothes, good shoes, a necktie, hat, and such. We could wear suits after working hours.

Some of the men didn't believe in the black market and tried to make money playing card games, like poker or Twenty-one. You have to be an expert to make money that way. Their table would be piled with money, even gold watches — special, expensive Swiss watches. They would cost about 500 Marks. Everyone could play. I played and lost the beautiful Swiss watches and some money. There was such a big pile of money on the table that the players' hands shook when they put money on the pile. The guards who weren't playing watched.

There was a good deal on American dollars in the black market. The Jewish buyers I dealt with had American money in piles. They also had good deals on English-made material for suits. The Jewish buyers had just about everything. You could even buy a car through them.

As a result of all this, the guards had beautiful suits, hats, shoes, and other clothes. They were so neatly dressed that they looked like executives. Our officers began to wonder why the guards were so well dressed, but not many paid much attention.

However, a Polish lieutenant named Rybok, our officer in the Second platoon, came to our barracks quite often. He tried to liquidate the games. He was probably jealous when he saw all that money on the table. He not only didn't want us to play cards, but he told the Polish captain, Olecha, about it. The captain didn't listen to him, though. So Rybok went to Duman, who also didn't pay much attention. He had something going on in that big German house where he lived. On weekdays, Duman was a devil, and he'd get mad at everyone. On the weekends, in the house, he was an angel. Other American officers would go by that house. There were about two dozen German girls there. They were sleeping together. All types of whiskey and beer were delivered to the door. This went on every weekend. The Polish company kitchen was very poor. There was hardly anything there to eat. Our food was going to Duman's big house.

Our company guards had received good evaluations for the work we'd done. We were rated better than satisfactory, but that didn't help us with our platoon lieutenant. Rybok was another devil and a stubborn bull. He had to find out why we guards were dressing better than he was. One day, Rybok brought in a barber who spoke Polish, English, and other languages. He would chat with the guards as he cut their hair. Masterniak and I figured out he was a spy right away. We put the word out to the other guards not to talk about the black market and that the barber was Rybok's spy. We quit the black market for a while, so the barber didn't help Rybok at all. We got free haircuts, though.

A few days later, a young man named Kuta joined our platoon. We started the black market again, and no one found out.

There were banks in town, but we didn't believe in them. We believed in big, glass pickle jars. We'd put the money in the jars, put the lids back on them, and bury them somewhere away from our post. The money was very safe in a jar. You just needed to mark where you buried it and make sure that no one saw you. The best time to do it was at night. Everybody spread out to find a good place to bury his jar. We wouldn't make with-drawals unless we were transferred or quit the company. This was the most trustworthy bank in the world.

From time to time in the company, guards would get promotions. I was in line to be a corporal because I'd been a good guard and because my English was good, something the officers liked.

Our platoon was subject to surprise inspections at any time of the day or night. We had just come back from midnight guard and settled in our beds, when officers came in. They said, "On your feet!" They searched us and the beds. In my wallet, they found a little money, but they couldn't hang me for that. On Masterniak, they found more money and the pistol. Masterniak usually kept the pistol outside, but tonight he had been so sleepy that he forgot to hide it out there. Rybok took Masterniak to Duman, who called the American and German police. They hauled Masterniak to jail. The next day, Kuta was taken to jail because he had a few Marks too many.

Both Masterniak and Kuta were very hard men to get something out of. We heard the police beat them up, but they said nothing. Some of the guards told our three buyers that we had to stop the black market. The two Jews got a lawyer who got Masterniak and Kuta out in no time. The Jewish buyers didn't want Masterniak and Kuta to identify them to the police.

Masterniak and Kuta came back to the company. Masterniak was supposed to be sent to another jail, but the Jewish buyers managed to get the case dismissed, so he stayed with the company.

About a week later, Masterniak packed his things and signed out. In town, he signed on with a special unit.

With all this commotion, my promotion to corporal went into the trash can. Another guard named Fijks got the one I was supposed to get. I knew right away that he was the man who turned us into the officers. One time at dinner, I called him a traitor in front of everyone in the kitchen.

I said, "You traitor. You're not going to get another stripe on your sleeve because we all know very well you turned us in. In Dachau, you helped a German Nazi go free through the court, and here you almost had everybody put in jail."

"I didn't do any of that," Fijks said, shaking and looking green.

The Nazi that Fijks helped was one of the scientists who experimented on people. In court, Fijks testified that the doctor was a very reasonable human being. Fijks was probably a Nazi himself. He told us when he came to the platoon that he came from the Poland after the war, and he knew both languages very well. I think he turned us in because we didn't want him in our black market. He smelled like a rat. Fijks disappeared a couple of weeks later and quit the company. He disappeared like a ghost.

So everything went back to being about as normal as it could be. We were going to town dancing, drinking beer and wine, and having fun with the girls. One night at the dance hall, an American soldier got mad. I don't know why, except maybe that he was drunk. He grabbed the girlfriend of one of the guards.

He danced with her and began to push her around. The guard, named John, said, "Hey! You're pushing my girl around!" The American took out a straight razor and tried to cut him. I was close by and grabbed the American's hand, but he managed to slice my shoulder. I dropped his hand, and he ran away through the door. The blade went right through my coat and shirt to the shoulder. I was bleeding.

For a while, with the blood loss, I thought I was going blind. John's girlfriend began to help me. We got my coat and shirt off, and she went to the bar to get bandages. The music had stopped, and everyone was going home. She stayed with me and bandaged my wound. Then, she put my coat over her arm, and I put my shirt on. The man from the bar called a taxi, and she rode with me to the hospital. The doctor put in some stitches. My eyes were OK, now. Boy! I was lucky that girl helped me. I don't know why, but it seemed all the German girls would help me in any kind of trouble, during and after the war.

The girl's name was Nina. She took care of me in the hospital, then she went home. I stayed in the hospital, and Nina came to visit me every day. She even brought me flowers. She also took my bloody jacket and shirt. She washed and ironed them. She sewed up the holes the razor had cut. Then, she took my pants and cleaned and pressed them, too. My friends from the company also visited me in the hospital. They told me that there was trouble with the black market. While making a deal with some other Polish guards, one of the Jewish dealers was shot by an American MP and the German police. The other Jew and the German got into their cars and disappeared. Nothing happened to the Polish guards. The shooting finished the black market for good.

When I got out of the hospital, I had to report to Duman. He wanted to know how the fight at the dance hall happened. "We were at the dance, and an American soldier tried to cut John with a straight razor. I tried to stop him, and he turned the blade on me."

Polish Captain Olecha and Lieutenant Rybok both said, "Stanislaus, you are expelled from the company."

Duman said, "Stanislaus, you can't fight American soldiers."

"Sir, I didn't try to fight with him. All I did was tell him to put the blade away, and he chopped me. I just tried to break up a fight, that's all. He almost cut the girl, and he was shoving her around."

I got to stay with the company after all, and I stayed out of fights.

I had two weeks of vacation coming. The word was that there was good skiing in the mountains around Garmisch-Partenkirchen. They allowed just so many men to go skiing. About fifteen of us got into an American truck, and we were driven to Garmisch-Partenkirchen. We had a very experienced German ski instructor. I had brought ski boots, and he gave me some skis and poles. Up on the mountain, I put the skis on, and the instructor talked to us about how to brake and stop. He then asked if anyone was experienced on skis. Half of the group said they were, but I had never been skiing before. I thought to myself how at home, I used to slide on my little ice skates down an icy hill. "I don't see why I can't do it with two big boards."

I picked out a spot where I could go down at high speed and then double back halfway up a hill. I would turn around carefully and go back to where I started. From then on, I was skiing like a pro. I knew how to brake, speed up, and how to stop in case of danger. We did this for a couple of weeks. When the Polish officers and Captain Duman came up to see us, they decided to hold a contest. The instructor set up a slalom course, just like a real Olympic contest.

The instructor said, "Stanislaus, you're going to be first."

I said, "Why me?"

He said, "I know you know how to ski. Don't give me that."

Many soldiers, sergeants, and officers were on that slope watching.

I lined up first on the mountain, with everyone behind me. The instructor was at the bottom of the slope, holding a stopwatch. I came down fast and went around all the flags well. After I was done, the instructor said I'd made good time. When everyone had run the course, the results came in. I was in first place. I was so happy I could have jumped in the air. I received a big book with all the good skiers' names in it. The instructor also signed the book.

He announced the results over a loudspeaker and added, "It's Stanislaus's first time on skis. I just can't believe he did this being on skis for the first time."

Everybody who was there shook my hands and congratulated me on what a good job I'd done.

We were staying in a chalet and had good beds to sleep in. The day after the contest, the instructor took four of us good skiers out by train. I don't know how many miles we traveled, but we saw many mountains. We got off the train and started to ski back to the chalet. We made jumps and skied across mountainsides. The instructor was with us all the way. We got back to the chalet just as it was getting dark. The trip was fun, but dangerous, too. Fortunately, we all got back safely after seeing many mountains and valleys. The last day we were there was a Saturday. In the evening, there was a big party at a German restaurant. There was plenty of good food, drinks, and, most important, a dance and a lot of girls to dance with. The next day, we hopped back on the truck and rode back to Munich and Alabama Company.

I had some more vacation coming to me, another two weeks. So right after the ski trip, I took Nina on a trip. We took the train to Chiemsee, a lake. We visited a castle that Ludwig II built for himself, which was open to tourists. We stayed at a resort hotel by the lake. The weather was gorgeous. We had a boat to ride around the lake and to go to the castle. When we toured the castle, we found it had golden knobs and curtains, and plenty of dust.

There was a moat around the castle. The lake also went right up to it. That's where the king used to go swimming. He would dive out of a special window in the castle right into the lake. We heard a story that the king's doctor had been told by the people to drown the king. They didn't like the way he was building new castles and hiking taxes. When they went out by boat one day, the doctor did drown the king, but the doctor drowned, too, when the boat sank.

Besides going to town, boating around the lake, and touring the castle, we went swimming every day. Nina taught me. The weather was sunny and beautiful, just right for it. In the evenings, we went dancing. There was a wonderful German dance band, with a violin, saxophone, trumpet, clarinet, piano, and drums.

One evening before bed, we went to take a bath because there were no showers. The hotel manager said, "There's only one bath, so you have to take turns." We both went into the bathtub, and we laughed and washed each other's back. We had a lot of fun, and we even had sex. The manager, a woman, knocked on the door.

"Who's there?" Nina said.

"Do you have two people in the bathtub?" the manager asked.

"Come on now!" Nina said sharply. "I'm in here alone."

"I heard two people talking in there," the manager said.

Nina said, "I heard some other people talking outside. Maybe that's what you heard."

When the manager left, Nina whispered, "I'll go first to the bedroom, unlock the door, and leave it open wide." She checked out the hall to see if anyone was coming, and said, "OK," in a whisper. "OK, Stanislaus, you can come now." No one was the wiser.

At this time, Nina suggested that we should get married. "It's a better life," she said. "This could be our honeymoon."

248

"We'll see how everything works out after we get home," I said. "After everything is straightened out, I'll probably marry you." Nina came from a prominent family in Germany. She had two children, Luke, who was nine years old, and girl named Mary, who was six. Her mother took care of them. I liked the children.

I asked Nina if her mother would have any objection to us getting married, and Nina answered, "No, she won't mind."

After the vacation, Nina told me that her husband was shot at the front. He was a major, but he was not a Nazi, she said. She was Catholic, and I visited her a lot. I slept at her apartment, which had a big, antique bed.

Nina and the children came with me to swim in the Isar river. It was clean and clear, with strong currents. Many people were there. Everybody sunned themselves on the bank.

I had already had a lot of chances to go to America. One day, I finally made up my mind to immigrate to the United States and went to the office to sign up.

Captain Duman had gone totally crazy. He gave everyone extra duty and extra hard work. He wanted the company to build a cement tennis court for him. I don't think they ever finished because everybody quit and told him to do it himself. From then on, everybody started signing up for immigration. The Polish organization in the United States helped us all come over or to go anywhere we wanted. Captain Olecha went to New York. Rybok went to Mississippi. Kuta went to Australia, and others went to South America and Canada.

After I signed up to immigrate, I dug up my money jar, I covered up the hole and left the empty jar on top. I spent all my German Marks before I left. I spent many of them on Nina because she deserved it for the way she helped me after that American cut me. I also spent money on my friends in the Polish guards.

I thought about marrying Nina and buying a business, but I was scared that after the Germans got on their feet, they would chase all the foreigners out of the country. Things were changing, and the Germans who cowered under the Nazis were beginning to forget. If you asked them who was to blame for the war, they'd say, "You must forget World War II because it is over, and Hitler is dead. It was only the madness of one man!"

You can't forget! Or let it go! It must be written in people's memories like arithmetic. We must slam a huge hammer on an anvil and let the sound travel around the world to all our children, carrying the message that we'll have a better world if we don't forget.

Nina and I had a few days together, and then I was told I had a plane ticket to the U.S. That meant Nina and I had to separate. "Maybe I can come back and bring you to the United States," I told her.

When it was time to get on the plane, Nina came to say goodbye. Just before I had to board, she said, "Write and tell me how you're doing over there, will you?" She gave me a little present, from around her own neck, a little golden chain and a cross. She put it around my neck. "This cross will guide you to a good life, Stanislaus."

I kissed her, thanked her, and hugged her hard. Then, kissed her again. I felt so sad to say goodbye, but this was it. I had to get on the plane headed for the United States.

OLYMPIA

I didn't marry any of the German girls — Rita, Guedraut, or Nina. In 1949, I met a Polish girl who had come from Siberia with the group that General Sikorski saved from Stalin. She had journeyed from Siberia to the Middle East, and, finally, to Mexico for safety. I married her in 1950. Her name was Olympia Barbara Dominiak.

STAN

I came from Germany on a B29 bomber. We landed in New York. I was among a group of immigrants from Germany who took a bus out to Long Island to work on a big farm. The farm was by the ocean. We lived in barracks there, and after work, we'd swim and bathe in the ocean. We worked every day, picking beans, cucumbers, and other vegetables from the fields.

From there I went to Batavia, New York, where I worked for a Polish farmer. I did the plowing, repaired cars, fed the animals, fertilized the fields, and drove tractors. I worked for him all winter.

A friend who had immigrated from Germany sent me a letter from Chicago that said, "Why don't you come to Chicago to work?" So I got on the train for Chicago, and he lined up a job for me at the Rohy Company, inspecting rubber seals. From then on, I was able to find a variety of jobs, each with better pay. I never went more than a week or two between jobs.

On August 27, 1950, I married Olympia Dominiak. Stalin's Red Army took her family from Wilno, Poland, to Siberia in 1939. In a deal with Polish General Sikorski, Stalin freed the Poles in Siberia after the Germans invaded the Soviet Union in July 1941. Olympia and her mother were sent to Mexico. Her father was sent to England to serve in the Polish Second Corps.

We rented a house in Chicago. We had a daughter, Jeannie. I worked as a punch-press operator. I also did some work patching furniture. We moved to a third-floor apartment in Chicago and had a son, Allen. All this time, I worked, and we bought a house. I was drafted for the Korean War, and we had another son, James. When I went through the induction process, I was deferred. Even so, I had to report to the Selective Service once a month until the end of the conflict.

I must have had about 50 jobs before I started to work at the Western Avenue railroad yard. I was carpenter first, then I was laid off and took another job at Chicago Union Station. I worked handling baggage, loading and unloading. I did that job for quite a while, then I become an elevator operator. After that, I became a ticket examiner. When the railroad switched to Amtrak, I automatically retained my position. I worked on the railroad thirty-three-and-a-half years. During that time, we had another son, Adrian.

I retired May 31, 1990. I stayed home taking care of my lovely wife, who was dying of cancer. On Saturday, July 14, 1990, my dear wife died. After her death, I sold my house in Franklin Park, Illinois, and moved to Waconia, Minnesota, where I lived for six years. Now, I live in Akely, Minnesota. I also spend five months of the year in Arizona.

Stanislaus Domoradzki
Born in Konczyce, Poland